SCHOLASTIC

Graphic Organizers & Strategy Sheets

That Scaffold Writing From Paragraphs to Essays

Anina Robb

New York • Toronto • London • Auckland • Sydney
Mexico City • New Delhi • Hong Kong • Buenos Aires

Teaching *Resources*

To my husband, Rob, and son, Lucas,
who give me time to write.

Cover design by Jorge J. Namerow
Interior design by Kelli Thompson
ISBN-13 978-0-439-82772-0
ISBN-10 0-439-82772-8

2 3 4 5 6 7 8 9 10   31   14 13 12 11 10 09 08 07

Contents

Introduction

When I was too young to hold a pencil, I used to pass the time on long car trips by spinning stories for my family—about princesses, goblins, and foxes. But it was only when I was finally old enough to hold a pencil and write words that my love affair with writing began. Early on, I was lucky to have a few teachers who understood good writing and loved writing themselves. Their sheer joy for words inspired me. They helped me generate ideas, organize ideas, write fluent sentences, use writing conventions properly, and find my voice. My teachers gave me the match, but my way into the writing fire took time, lots of time. So often in language arts classes there is so much to "do"—that time to think, brainstorm, write, crumple up the paper and begin again does not exist. But time is what students need when writing. The process cannot be rushed. Writing comes more easily to some than to others, but all children have something to say in words.

Writing is a process. It involves many stages and missteps—and considerable time. Sometimes you jump a stage in the process only to come back to it later. Sometimes you linger on a stage longer than you had anticipated. As the teacher, you can help your students become writers by doing several things:

- Give students many opportunities to evaluate and critique writing. That is, let them tell you what makes a piece of writing good or worth reading—and where it needs improvement.
- Provide a range of writing samples for them to read. Giving students the opportunity to respond to and assess many kinds of writing—from professionals to peers—is invaluable.
- Use rubrics. Make sure there is no magic or guesswork about your expectations for a piece of writing. Give students the opportunity to meet the criteria you've set for each assignment.

Ultimately, we want students to learn how to talk about writing, think like writers, and embrace the writing process. The lessons I've compiled in this book are designed to target the prewriting, writing, revising, and editing stages of writing. They provide models of great writing that students can respond to, and they are designed to coach them along as they plan, draft, and reshape their work. Best of all, students work independently so they can progress at their own pace, taking the time they need in order to develop as writers.

Motivating Young Writers

"I have nothing to write about," "I'm done," "I like it the way it is!" These voices are commonly heard in a writing classroom. With everything battling for their attention these days—the computer, cell phones, and video games—many students have become numbed to their senses, disengaged. Reading and then writing about the world will help reconnect these students to their ideas—and the possibility of diving deeper into their ideas. The lessons in this book present interesting models and encourage students to write about their interests. The approach engages students in an exploration of a variety of writing formats—from descriptive paragraphs to persuasive essays—that they will use in school and beyond.

A Realistic Approach to Teaching the Writing Process

Wouldn't it be nice if you could have students just spurt out an essay on a moment's notice? The majority of writing does not happen in a flash of inspiration. It comes from hard work; it comes from process. The traditional writing process is broken down into these five stages:

Prewriting—a creative time to develop ideas for writing and consider structures for the writing

Writing—the experimenting and shaping phase for writing ideas down as a draft

Revising—the time to narrow the focus of the writing and clarify ideas

Editing—correcting and polishing the work so that it meets the standards of English

Publishing—making the finished copy ready for display or presentation

Often teachers present the writing process to their students as if it happens in this neat, stepping stone–like way. In the real world it does not—writing is much more complicated than that. If you can help students understand this, they might be less afraid of the process.

When you teach writing, show students how you move back and forth between the stages.

- Plan to spend a lot of time on prewriting techniques, such as webbing, brainstorming, visualizing, developing questions, and outlining. As you do so, dabble in the drafting stage. For instance, I like to model for my students how I jot down new ideas sparked by my prewriting. I explain that when an idea comes, I always listen to that idea and write about it immediately—even if eventually the idea goes nowhere—because this exploratory writing generates more writing.
- While you are modeling writing for the class, talk about how you are also revising as you go—you may cross out words, draw arrows, add ideas, and think about moving paragraphs around, even in the first draft.
- While rewriting, you might notice that you've forgotten to capitalize the first word of a sentence. Show students how you take a moment to attend to conventions even before the final draft—that is editing!

Certainly we need to help students understand that writing is a process, but let's not lock them into a rigid model. Let's show them how writers enter and exit these stages according to their writing needs.

Using This Book

This book includes 23 short lessons that cover a variety of formats and skills students need to master in both fiction and nonfiction writing.

The lessons are organized into four sections. Chapter 1 offers lessons on writing the lead and the conclusion to help students frame every piece of writing. The lessons in Chapters 2 and 3 focus on nonfiction and narrative writing respectively and progress from paragraphs to longer formats, such as essays and short stories. The lessons in Chapter 4 target skills in revising and editing.

With each lesson, you'll find writing pages that coach students to work independently. These pages help guide independent writing instruction in three ways:

1. by focusing on the writing process so that students develop the skills they need to do all kinds of writing across the curriculum
2. by providing students with a way to evaluate their own writing
3. by serving as a built-in structure for you to manage an independent writing program in your classroom

It is not necessary for students to complete the activity pages in every lesson. Plan to use this book as if it were a menu—pick and choose the lessons that will nourish each student and meet your goals for the curricula.

When you decide on a lesson, make sure you have modeled for students the type of writing featured in the lesson. Then have students who are ready try writing on their own with the independent-activity sheets. The first few times students work with the activity pages, review the instructions before sending them off to write. Invite students to pose questions that will help clarify the assignment. As students become more confident writing a certain genre or format, you can pair them with others who need more support.

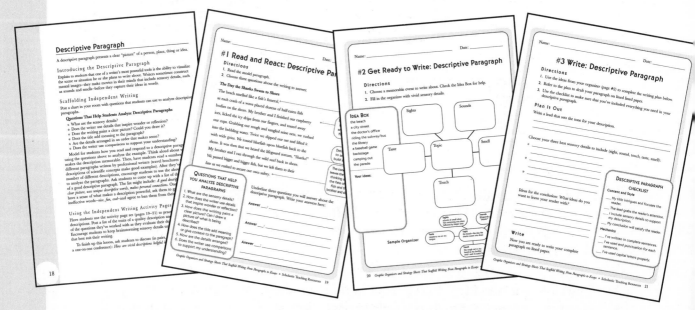

Each lesson includes a page of instruction ideas and a set of three or four reproducible pages that guide students through the writing process—from critiquing a model and prewriting to drafting, revising, and editing.

Assessment

A checklist at the end of each lesson provides a simple way for students to check that they've included key elements in their writing. You may also want to develop a rubric for the writing (see pages 108–109) to spell out more detailed criteria. Make sure that students understand that the checklist and rubric are provided so that the grading criteria are not a mystery. Their grade will be determined according to how well they have met these expectations.

Here are some common issues to watch for and address as you read students' writing:

- The writing is general. If a student's writing lacks specific details or examples, chances are he or she did not spend time prewriting. Give them an opportunity to generate more ideas with a partner or independently with a prewriting tool such as a web.

- The writing is disorganized. Ask students why the writing is not organized. It might be that the student was overwhelmed with ideas or did not understand how to organize his or her thoughts. Help students understand what they need to do by working to create an outline or visual map of the piece and then give them time to rewrite.

- The writing is not clear. Have students read aloud what they have written. Ask them to add more details and "rewrite" parts orally to you. When they can use speech to express their ideas, they can write down the revisions. You might have to model what a clear response sounds like before asking students to rewrite their unclear writing.

● ● ● ●

Now that you're familiar with the content and structure of this book, I hope you enjoy selecting the lessons that meet your students' needs and adapting the materials as you see fit to make independent writing a success in your classroom.

CHAPTER 1

Writing the Beginning and the Ending

For many writers—even professional writers—figuring out what to write about is the hardest part of the writing process. Often, when student writers finally have a good idea to pursue, they struggle with putting their thoughts together into one clear opening idea that frames the rest of the writing—the lead. To emphasize the importance of the lead, I tell my students, "In sports, a good kick-off starts the game off right. In writing, a good lead should 'kick off' your writing." Furthermore, the lead must be engaging enough to pull the reader into the writing. I often spend a week working on leads with students. We focus on these three aspects: the lead is narrow enough but not too narrow, the lead sparks the reader's interest, and the lead commits to a certain voice or tone.

To help students, create a poster with these tips:

- Begin with a funny story or quote.
- Challenge the reader with a question.
- Tease the reader with a bit of your conclusion.
- List all of your main points in a serious way.
- Come up with a new angle or way of looking at a topic.

Students may find the conclusion just as daunting to write as the lead. Sometimes, the conclusion happens naturally and writers come to a genuine stopping place, but at other times, the writer has to make important choices about how to close his or her piece. Teach students that conclusions accomplish these main goals:

1. tie up loose ends
2. clarify parts of your writing
3. keep the reader thinking

I tell students that a good conclusion is important because it helps the reader understand these things: what they have read, why it is important, and what they should do about it. In order to get these three things into their conclusions, students can use this simple formula when they first write conclusions: Restate your central idea by using one of the devices that help you write a lead (for example, a question, an anecdote, or a restating of facts).

> **Lessons in This Section**
>
> - The Lead
> - The Conclusion

The Lead

A lead invites the reader into the piece. It can be the first sentence of a paragraph or an entire paragraph in an essay. The lead prepares the reader for what will come next.

Introducing Leads

Introduce students to the concept of the lead by asking what they would do if they read a first sentence in an article or story that was "blah"–boring. They would probably answer, "I wouldn't read on" or "I'd set it down." Explain that because a lead often tells what the paragraph will be about, writing an interesting lead sentence that grabs the reader's attention is very important. You might compare the lead to the engine on a train. It is the main idea that all the other cars–or sentences–are attached to.

Scaffolding Independent Writing

Post a chart in your room with questions students can use to analyze leads.

Questions That Help Students Analyze Leads

- What did you learn the piece was about?
- What did the author do that grabbed you?
- What made the lead boring or interesting?
- What ideas in the lead made you wonder?
- What details does the lead include?
- How could this lead be improved?

Model for students how you read and respond to a lead, using the questions above to analyze a well-written example. Think aloud about what makes the lead a good lead. Then have students read different leads–they can vary from one sentence to an opening paragraph and may be fiction or nonfiction leads, depending on your focus. Encourage students to use the questions above to analyze the leads. Ask students to come up with a list of traits that a good lead has. The list might include: *raises questions that make you wonder, contains an anecdote that fascinates, creates a mood, presents new information, introduces an unusual setting,* and *has action that intrigues.*

Using the Independent Writing Activity Pages

Have students use the activity page set (pages 10–12) to practice writing their own attention-grabbing leads. Post the list of traits for a quality lead and remind students of the questions they've asked as they evaluate the leads. At the end of the activity, students will have a strong, revised lead. Encourage students to write two or three variations of the lead until they find the one that best suits their writing.

To finish up this lesson, ask students to discuss (in pairs, as a whole class, or in a one-on-one conference): *What makes a good lead*

Name: _____   Date: _____

#1 Read and React: The Lead

Directions

1. Read the model lead.
2. Circle the details you liked in the writing.
3. Choose three questions about the writing to answer.

Lead for a Personal Essay

I could hear my dad saying, "Don't leave the cat's food out all night!" but I wanted to lure the stray cat to our back porch so I could make him my own. When I thought I heard the cat scratching at the milk bowl, I peered out the back door only to find a beady-eyed rodent staring back at me. "It's a rat!" I screamed.

> The first sentence opens the piece with the narrator breaking the rules to get what she wants—a great way to hook a reader.

> The writer shows the fear that she felt when she saw the opossum.

QUESTIONS THAT HELP YOU ANALYZE LEADS

1. Did you learn what the piece is about?
2. What made the lead boring?
3. What in the lead grabbed your attention?
4. What left you wondering and wanting to read on?
5. What sensory details are in the lead?
6. What changes would make it better?

Underline three questions you will answer about the sample lead. Write your answers here:

Answer ___: _____

_____

_____

Answer ___: _____

_____

_____

Answer ___: _____

_____

_____

Name: _____ Date: _____

#2 Get Ready to Write: The Lead

Directions

1. Choose a topic to write about. Check the Idea Box for help.

2. Fill in the organizer with descriptive details to help you write a paragraph with a strong lead.

IDEA BOX

picking apples

how airplanes fly

first haircut

lies and friends

trying out for the team

caring for a sick pet

family party

Your ideas:

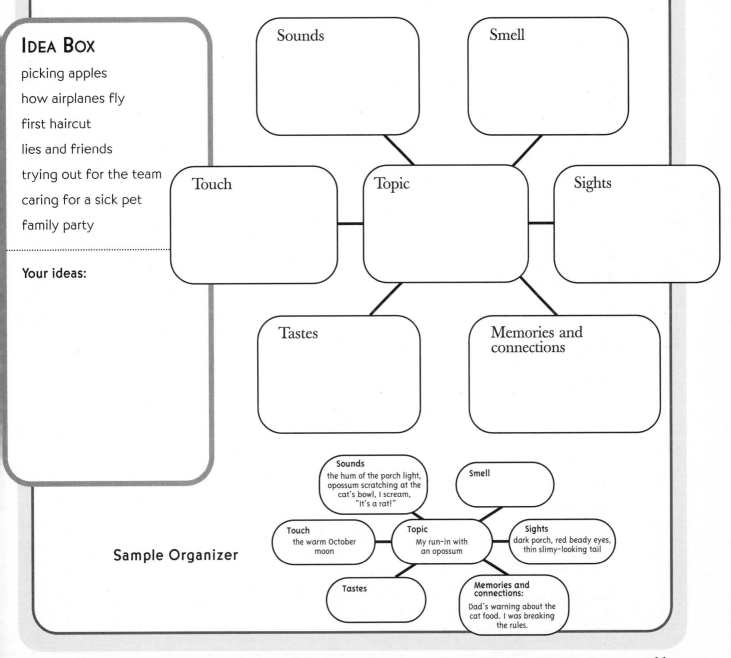

Sounds

Smell

Touch

Topic

Sights

Tastes

Memories and connections

Sample Organizer

Sounds
the hum of the porch light, opossum scratching at the cat's bowl, I scream, "It's a rat!"

Smell

Touch
the warm October moon

Topic
My run-in with an opossum

Sights
dark porch, red beady eyes, thin slimy-looking tail

Tastes

Memories and connections:
Dad's warning about the cat food. I was breaking the rules.

Name: _____   Date: _____

#3 Write: The Lead

Directions

1. Write your first draft lead.
2. Rewrite your lead using the tips below.
3. Use the checklist to make sure you've included all your ideas and polished the writing.

Writing a First Draft

Use the best ideas you came up with in your organizer to write a lead:

_____

_____

_____

_____

(Tip!) Strengthening a Lead

Sample lead sentence:
The balloon goes up.

Sample lead sentence revised:
The balloon races into the sky.

Think: How did the revised sentence make you sense the movement of the balloon? Instead of *goes*, a writer can try stronger, more precise verbs, such as *speeds*, *wanders*, *zooms*, and *dashes*.

What other strong verbs could you add to this list in place of *goes*?

_____, _____, _____, _____

What strong verbs could you add in your first draft lead?

_____, _____, _____, _____

LEADS CHECKLIST

Content and Style

____ The lead grabs my reader's attention.

____ The lead introduces the topic I'm writing about.

____ I use sensory details.

____ My verbs are exact and strong.

Mechanics

____ I use a period, question mark, or exclamation point to end each sentence.

Revising Your Lead

Use these ideas to revise your first draft lead on lined paper.

The Conclusion

The conclusion, or closing, may sum up information in the paragraph or tell what it means. It can reflect on the lead or thesis, review the main points, answer unresolved questions, direct the reader to take action, or connect the paragraph's content to the reader's experience.

Introducing Conclusions

Ask students to describe how they would feel if they had to leave a movie ten minutes before the end, or stop reading a book just before the final chapter. Follow up by asking students, *What is the purpose of an ending* Refer to their responses—for example, that loose ends are tied up, problems are solved, or a purpose is revealed—in describing the role a conclusion plays in a piece of writing.

Scaffolding Independent Writing

Post a chart in your room with questions students can use to analyze conclusions.

Questions That Help Students Analyze Conclusions

- Does it tie up loose ends?
- Does it refer to a lead or thesis?
- Does it review the main points?
- Does it call upon the reader to take action?
- Does it connect with the reader's experience?

Model for students how you read and respond to a conclusion, using the questions above to analyze the example. Think aloud about what makes a conclusion satisfying. Next, have students read a number of different conclusions written by professional writers and encourage them to use the questions above to analyze the writing. Finally, ask students to come up with a list of the elements of a good conclusions. The list might include: *sums up information, refers back to the lead,* and *inspires action.*

Using the Independent Writing Activity Pages

Have students use the activity page set (14–16) to practice writing conclusions. Post the list of the traits of a quality conclusion and remind students of the questions they've asked as they evaluate their conclusions. Encourage students to write two or three variations of the conclusion until they find the one that best suits their writing. At the end of the activity, students will have a strong, revised conclusion.

To finish up this lesson, ask students to discuss (in pairs, as a whole class, or in a one-on-one conference): *Why is it important to add a good closing to any piece of writing*

#1 Read and React: The Conclusion

Directions

1. Read the model paragraph.

2. Choose three questions about the conclusion to answer.

Persuasive Paragraph With Conclusion

According to nutritionists, people need to eat frequently—
every two to three hours—in order to stay energetic and
alert. However, like many of my classmates, I have breakfast
around 6:30 am, a full six hours before my scheduled school
lunch time. By 10:15 my stomach's growl can be heard above
the teacher's voice: "FEED ME!" Distracted by all the
rumbling, I inevitably lose focus on my schoolwork and
sometimes even doze off. Allowing students like me
five minutes to satisfy their hunger will, in the end,
give teachers hours of more productive classroom time.
Students, parents, and teachers should all be aware
that scientific evidence supports the need for a mid-morning
snack. This is an issue worth speaking up about—it really
does affect learning!

Conclusion

QUESTIONS THAT HELP YOU ANALYZE CONCLUSIONS

1. How does the conclusion tie up loose ends?
2. How does it refer to a lead or thesis?
3. How does it review the main points?
4. How does it call upon the reader to take action?
5. How does it connect with the reader's experience?

Underline three questions you will answer about the conclusion. Write your answers here:

Answer ___: _____

_____

Answer ___: _____

_____

Answer ___: _____

_____

Name: _____   Date: _____

#2 Get Ready to Write: The Conclusion

Directions

1. Choose a topic to write about. Check the Idea Box for help.
2. Use the organizer to help you generate ideas for your paragraph.

IDEA BOX

how to get ready for school

what I like about my favorite sport

an inspirational person

a powerful thunderstorm

a memorable bus ride

Your ideas:

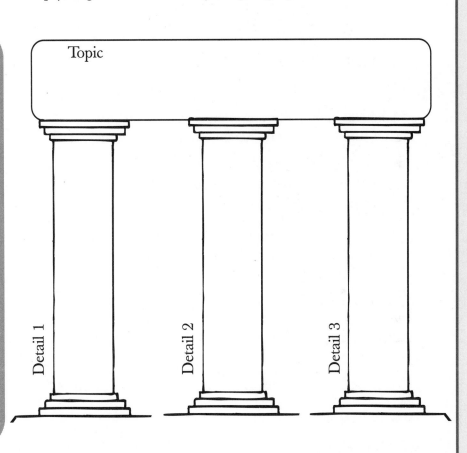

Topic

Detail 1

Detail 2

Detail 3

After reading my paragraph, I want my reader to:

_____

_____

_____

_____

_____

_____

Sample Organizer

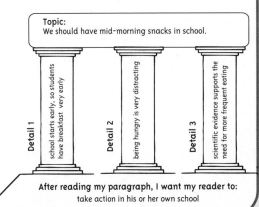

Topic:
We should have mid-morning snacks in school.

Detail 1 — school starts early, so students have breakfast very early

Detail 2 — being hungry is very distracting

Detail 3 — scientific evidence supports the need for more frequent eating

After reading my paragraph, I want my reader to:
take action in his or her own school

#3 Write: The Conclusion

Directions

1. Use the ideas from your organizer (page #2) to write a first draft of your paragraph on lined paper. Add a concluding sentence that serves the purpose you stated in your organizer. (See the tip below to strengthen your conclusion.)

2. Make any revisions and copy the paragraph below.

3. Use the checklist to make sure you've included all your ideas and polished the writing.

Strengthening a Conclusion

Tip! Here are three kinds of conclusions writers use. Which works best for your paragraph?

Sum Up: Think of your ending as a chance to sum up what you have written or reinforce your main point.

Call to Action: Inspire the reader to take action based on what you've written.

Connect to the Reader's Experience: Help the reader understand how what you've written about applies to his or her life.

Try one here: _____

_____

_____

_____

_____

_____

_____

CONCLUSION CHECKLIST

Content and Style

___ I wrap up my ideas in the conclusion.

___ I do one of these in my conclusion: sum up the writing, call the reader to take action, or connect the writing to the reader's own experiences.

___ My verbs are exact and strong.

Mechanics

___ I use a period, question mark, or exclamation point to end each sentence.

Write

Choose the best conclusion and write your paragraph below.

_____

_____

_____

_____

_____

CHAPTER 2

Writing Nonfiction

Nonfiction writers are often faced with this problem: *I have so much information to share! How should I write it*

The lessons in this section provide students with a framework for the different structures of nonfiction writing. Remind students of the importance of this kind of writing by pointing out that for a history project, they may need to write an essay about the causes and effects of a certain war; in science, they may need to write an essay about how a complex system works; and for writing contests and applications, they may be asked to write about a personal experience that changed their lives. All of this writing falls under the term *nonfiction*.

The best nonfiction writing happens when a writer sounds as if he or she really knows the topic—the words read authoritatively. It also helps if the writing flows logically and clearly from one idea to the next.

The organizers and strategy sheets that follow encourage students to think and collect ideas before diving into writing to find interesting content. The sheets also help students pace their writing and take responsibility for using the writing process.

To help students, create a poster with these tips to hang in your room:

- Start building interesting ideas for writing: Gather and organize your thoughts.
- Set a purpose: Are you presenting information? Are you comparing and contrasting?
- Follow the format for the kind of writing you've chosen: State your topic early and organize your ideas in a structured way.
- Write for your audience: Are you writing for your teacher, your friends, the news? Adjust your presentation to hook these specific readers.
- Choose your writing voice: Most nonfiction writing uses a semiformal voice that sounds fairly serious and reliable. Make sure your voice stays consistent throughout.

Lessons in This Section

Paragraphs
- Descriptive
- Persuasive
- Sequence
- Expository

Longer Formats
- Personal Essay
- Persuasive Essay
- Informative Essay
- News Article

Descriptive Paragraph

A descriptive paragraph presents a clear "picture" of a person, place, thing, or idea.

Introducing the Descriptive Paragraph

Explain to students that one of a writer's most powerful tools is the ability to visualize the scene or situation he or she plans to write about. Writers sometimes construct mental images—they make movies in their minds that include sensory details, such as sounds and smells—before they capture their ideas in words.

Scaffolding Independent Writing

Post a chart in your room with questions that students can use to analyze descriptive paragraphs.

Questions That Help Students Analyze Descriptive Paragraphs

- What are the sensory details?
- Does the writer use details that inspire wonder or reflection?
- Does the writing paint a clear picture? Could you draw it?
- Does the title add meaning to the paragraph?
- Are the details arranged in an order that makes sense?
- Does the writer use comparisons to support your understanding?

Model for students how you read and respond to a descriptive paragraph, using the questions above to analyze the example. Think aloud about what makes the description memorable. Then, have students read a number of different paragraphs written by professional writers (travel brochures or clear descriptions of scientific concepts make good examples). After they've read a number of different descriptions, encourage students to use the above questions to analyze the paragraphs. Ask students to come up with a list of the elements of a good descriptive paragraph. The list might include: *paints a clear picture, uses unique descriptive words*, and *makes personal connections*. Once students have a sense of what makes a description powerful, ask them to generate a list of ineffective words—*nice, fun, cool*—and agree to ban them from their writing.

Using the Independent Writing Activity Pages

Have students use the activity page set (pages 19–21) to practice writing descriptions. Post a list of the traits of a quality description and remind students of the questions they've worked with as they evaluate their descriptive paragraphs. Encourage students to keep brainstorming sensory details until they find the ones that best suit their writing.

To finish up this lesson, ask students to discuss (in pairs, as a whole class, or in a one-on-one conference): *How are vivid descriptions helpful in nonfiction writing*

#1 Read and React: Descriptive Paragraph

Directions

1. Read the model paragraph.
2. Choose three questions about the writing to answer.

The Day the Sharks Swam to Shore

The beach smelled like a fish's funeral, as each crash of a wave placed dozens of half-eaten fish bodies on the shore. My brother and I finished our raspberry ices, licked the icy drips from our fingers, and tossed away our cups. Grabbing our rough and tangled seine nets, we rushed into the bubbling water. Twice we dipped our net and lifted it with wide grins. We tossed bluefish upon bluefish back to the shore. It was then that we heard the lifeguard scream, "Sharks!" My brother and I ran through the wild surf back to shore. We passed bigger and bigger fish, but we left them to their fate as we rushed to secure our own safety.

> The title sets the scene.

> The lead sets the tone ("funeral" and "half-eaten fish bodies").

> Details appeal to senses and build suspense.

> The conclusion leaves the reader thinking about the fate of the fish and the brother and sister.

QUESTIONS THAT HELP YOU ANALYZE DESCRIPTIVE PARAGRAPHS

1. What are the sensory details?
2. How does the writer use details that inspire wonder or reflection?
3. How does the writing paint a clear picture? Can I draw a picture of what is being described?
4. How does the title add meaning or give context to the paragraph?
5. How are the details arranged?
6. Does the writer use comparisons to support my understanding?

Underline three questions you will answer about the descriptive paragraph. Write your answers here:

Answer ___: _____

_____

Answer ___: _____

_____

Answer ___: _____

_____

Name: _____   Date: _____

#2 Get Ready to Write: Descriptive Paragraph

Directions

1. Choose a memorable event to write about. Check the Idea Box for help.
2. Fill in the organizer with vivid sensory details.

IDEA BOX
the beach
a city street
the doctor's office
riding the subway/bus
the library
a baseball game
backstage
camping out
the parade

Your ideas:

Sights		Sounds

Taste	Topic	Smell

Touch

Sample Organizer

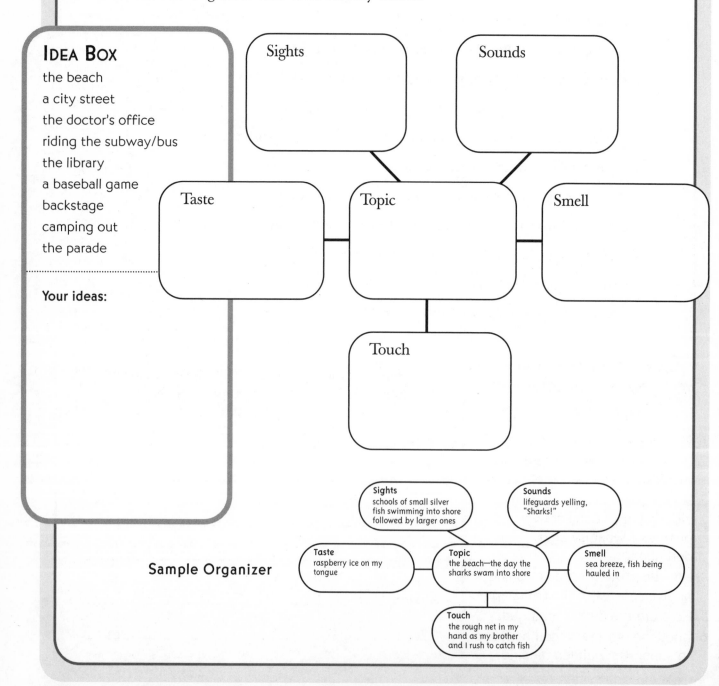

Sights
schools of small silver
fish swimming into shore
followed by larger ones

Sounds
lifeguards yelling,
"Sharks!"

Taste
raspberry ice on my
tongue

Topic
the beach—the day the
sharks swam into shore

Smell
sea breeze, fish being
hauled in

Touch
the rough net in my
hand as my brother
and I rush to catch fish

Name: _____ Date: _____

#3 Write: Descriptive Paragraph

Directions

1. Use the ideas from your organizer (page #2) to complete the writing plan below.

2. Refer to the plan to draft your paragraph on lined paper.

3. Use the checklist to make sure that you've included everything you need in your descriptive paragraph.

Plan It Out

Write a lead that sets the tone for your description.

_____

_____

Choose your three best sensory details to include (sight, sound, touch, taste, smell):

- _____

  _____

- _____

  _____

- _____

  _____

Ideas for the conclusion: What ideas do you want to leave your reader with?

_____

_____

_____

_____

Write

Now you are ready to write your complete paragraph on lined paper.

DESCRIPTIVE PARAGRAPH CHECKLIST

Content and Style

____ My title intrigues and focuses the reader.

____ The lead grabs the reader's attention.

____ I include sensory details to support my description.

____ My conclusion will satisfy the reader.

Mechanics

____ I've written in complete sentences.

____ I've used end punctuation for each sentence.

____ I've used capital letters properly.

Persuasive Paragraph

A persuasive paragraph expresses an opinion and tries to convince the reader that the opinion is valid.

Introducing the Persuasive Paragraph

Ask students to think of a time they tried to convince their parents (or another adult) of something, and to reflect on the strategies they used. Did they state their opinions clearly? Give reasons? Make comparisons? How did they respond to their parents' opposition? Explain to students that persuasive writing supports a cause, expresses an opinion, or makes an argument. A well-composed persuasive essay will be made up of three parts: the viewpoint, details supporting the viewpoint, and the presentation of an opposing argument, which is then refuted.

Scaffolding Independent Writing

Post a chart in your room with questions that students can use to analyze persuasive paragraphs.

Questions That Help Students Analyze Persuasive Paragraphs

- What is the author's viewpoint? Is it clear?
- Does the author present his or her opinion logically?
- Did the author make use of facts, observations, comparisons, or data to support his or her viewpoint?
- Is an opposing argument mentioned? How is it used?
- Did the author sway your opinion?
- How could the author's arguments be improved?

Model for students how you read and respond to a persuasive paragraph, using the questions above to analyze the example. Think aloud about what makes the argument persuasive. Next, have students read a number of different persuasive pieces written by professional writers. Scholastic *Action* or Scholastic *Scope* magazines are excellent resources. In addition, have students read editorials in newspapers or magazines, ideally reflecting different perspectives on the same topic.

After they've read a number of different persuasive pieces, encourage students to use the questions above to analyze selected paragraphs. Ask them to come up with a list of the elements of a good persuasive paragraph. The list might include: *a strong point of view, convincing supporting details, use of an opposing argument,* and *organizing the arguments logically.*

Using the Independent Writing Activity Pages

Have students use the activity page set (pages 23–25) to practice writing persuasive paragraphs. Post the list of the traits of a quality persuasive paragraph and remind students of the questions they worked with to evaluate the persuasive paragraphs. Encourage students to brainstorm more supporting details than they need, then select the most effective ones to include in the paragraph.

To finish up this lesson, ask students to discuss (in pairs, as a whole class, or in a one-on-one conference): *What techniques does the author use to support his or her argument Where was the strongest point placed*

#1 Read and React: Persuasive Paragraph

Directions

1. Read the model paragraph.

2. Choose two questions about the writing to answer.

Middle School Needs a New Start •————————————

> The title focuses the reader and helps set up the argument.

"Preteens and teens need more sleep and get better quality sleep in the morning," sleep expert Dr. Elizabeth Rich told me during a telephone conversation about whether middle schools should start the school day later. Dr. Rich explained that teenagers have a different rhythm to their sleep. By nature, teens stay up late and sleep late in the morning. Though schools have always begun early, teachers could also benefit from a later start to the school day: Students wouldn't be tardy or falling asleep in their morning classes. I know that I perform better when I am fully rested and awake. Students could improve their test scores and make school more enjoyable.

> A quote from an expert presents solid data to get the reader's attention and earn his or her trust.

> Scientific facts support the argument.

> Here is the opposite side of the argument with a counterargument.

> Personal experience reinforces the argument.

Pushing back the start time of middle school will improve students' ability to learn and allow teachers to reach students all day long. Sending a letter to parents or publishing an editorial in the newspaper would be a great way to explain to people why starting school at 9:30 a.m. would increase students' productivity and success.

> The conclusion sums up the points of the argument and offers a solution.

QUESTIONS THAT HELP YOU ANALYZE PERSUASIVE PARAGRAPHS

1. What is the author's viewpoint? Is it clear?

2. Does the author present his or her opinion logically? How?

3. How does the author make use of facts, observations, comparisons, or data to support his or her viewpoint?

4. Is an opposing argument mentioned? How is it used?

5. How did the author sway your opinion?

6. How could the author's arguments be improved?

Underline two questions you will answer about the persuasive paragraph. Write your answers on the back of the page.

Name: _____ Date: _____

#2 Get Ready to Write: Persuasive Paragraph

Directions

1. Choose a topic to write about that really matters to you. Check the Idea Box for help.

2. Fill in the organizer with supporting points. *Hint:* Do some research on your topic in the library or using reliable Internet sources, or contact an expert.

IDEA BOX

school uniforms

homework

whether computer games or movies encourage violence

....

Your ideas:

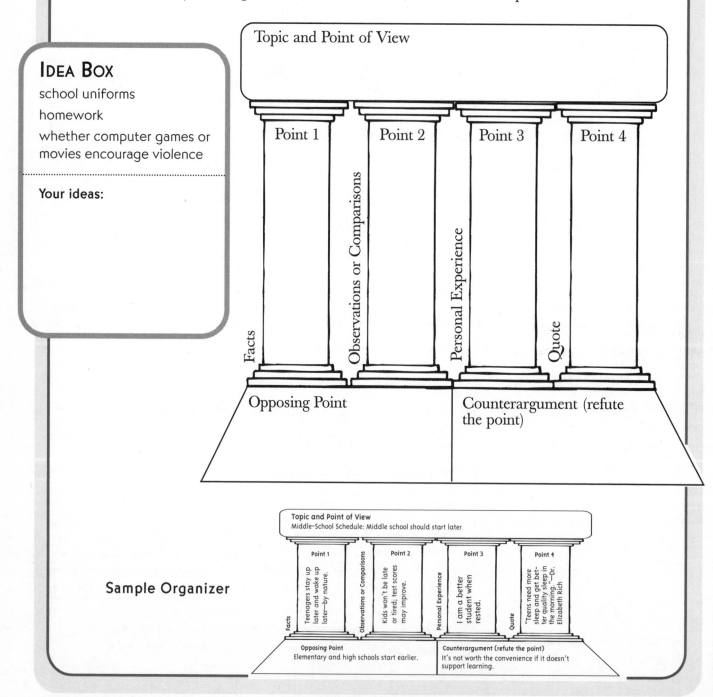

Topic and Point of View

Point 1 — Facts

Point 2 — Observations or Comparisons

Point 3 — Personal Experience

Point 4 — Quote

Opposing Point

Counterargument (refute the point)

Sample Organizer

Topic and Point of View
Middle-School Schedule: Middle school should start later

Point 1 — Facts: Teenagers stay up later and wake up later—by nature.

Point 2 — Observations or Comparisons: Kids won't be late or tired; test scores may improve.

Point 3 — Personal Experience: I am a better student when rested.

Point 4 — Quote: "Teens need more sleep and get better quality sleep in the morning."—Dr. Elizabeth Rich

Opposing Point: Elementary and high schools start earlier.

Counterargument (refute the point): It's not worth the convenience if it doesn't support learning.

Graphic Organizers and Strategy Sheets That Scaffold Writing From Paragraphs to Essays • Scholastic Teaching Resources

Name: _____ Date: _____

#3 Write: Persuasive Paragraph

Directions

1. Complete the writing plan below with ideas from your organizer (page #2).

2. Use the plan and tip below to draft your paragraph on lined paper.

3. Use the checklist to make sure that you've included everything you need in your persuasive paragraph.

Plan It Out

Possible title:

_____

_____

Possible lead:

_____

_____

_____

_____

Most important argument:

_____

_____

_____

_____

_____

PERSUASIVE PARAGRAPH CHECKLIST

Content and Style

___ My title intrigues and focuses the reader.

___ The lead makes my point of view clear.

___ I include facts or details to prove my point.

___ I've included an opposing argument.

___ My conclusion reinforces my opinion.

___ I've used powerful verbs.

Mechanics

___ I've written in complete sentences and used end punctuation.

___ I've used capital letters properly.

Tip!
In a persuasive paragraph, writers often put their strongest point at the beginning or end to pack a punch. The most convincing arguments include facts, data, research, and quotes from experts.

Possible conclusion (What do you want the reader to do after reading your arguments?):

_____

_____

Write

Now you are ready to write your complete paragraph on lined paper.

Sequence Paragraph

A sequence paragraph describes how a process works, or how to do something in a particular order. For example, it might explain how laws are made, or give directions on how to play a game, plant a garden, set up a tent, or walk from one place to another. Explanations in these paragraphs are precise and are organized in sequence.

Introducing the Sequence Paragraph

Ask students to explain the meaning of the term *chronological order*. Using their language and examples in your answer, tell students that they will be writing a paragraph that explains events or processes in the order in which they actually occur. Then, ask students what they've observed about how writers indicate time. Answers may include *giving the actual time, dates, hints about seasons, time of day*. Students may also point out that certain words, such as *previously*, *during*, and *until*, indicate sequence. These are time-order words.

Scaffolding Independent Writing

Post a chart in your room with questions that students can use to analyze sequence paragraphs.

Questions That Help Students Analyze Sequence Paragraphs

- Is the order of events clear?
- What time-order words or phrases does the writer use?
- If the paragraph describes a task, are the instructions clear?
- What did the writer do to keep your attention?
- What steps did you think were not clear?
- What would make the steps or instructions clearer?

Model for students how you read and respond to a sequence paragraph, using the questions above to analyze a well-written example. Pair up students and ask them to search a variety of sources (cookbooks, science textbooks, and written instructions are all good resources) for examples of sequence paragraphs. Call on three pairs of students to read a paragraph aloud and analyze it using the questions above. Then ask the class to generate a list of the elements of a good sequence paragraph. The list might include: *clear writing*, *use of time-order words*, and *ordering the sequence by steps or in time*.

After they've read a number of different well-sequenced pieces, brainstorm a list of time-order words with students and post it on a wall. Leave a marker hanging beside the chart so students can add more words as they think of them or come across them in their reading. Students can use the chart as a reference as they write.

Using the Independent Writing Activity Pages

Have students use the activity page set (pages 27–29) to practice writing sequence paragraphs. Encourage them to refer to the list of traits of good sequence paragraphs, questions for analyzing sequence paragraphs, and the list of time-order words.

To finish up this lesson, ask students to discuss (in pairs, as a whole class, or in a one-on-one conference): *Was the paragraph successful in describing the sequence or providing instruction to the reader Why Why not*

Name: _____ Date: _____

#1 Read and React: Sequence Paragraph

Directions

1. Read the model paragraph.
2. Choose three questions about the writing to answer.

A Full Circle Cycle

Water is recycled through the ecosystem, which is all the living things in a place. The path water takes through an ecosystem is called the water cycle. The water cycle happens in several steps. It starts with liquid water, or rain, falling to the earth from clouds. Water from rain soaks into the soil and falls into streams and lakes. The water then flows into the rivers and oceans. Eventually, water evaporates into the air again from the ground surface, from bodies of water, and from the leaves of plants. The water vapor in the air then helps to form new clouds. Clouds rise, become cool, and the water vapor condenses once again to become liquid water. Then the cycle begins again.

> This playful title draws the reader into a serious piece.

> A clearly stated fact introduces the paragraph.

> Prepares the reader for steps—and the beginning of the process.

> Clear statements in order explain the process.

> The conclusion comes full circle to restate the main idea.

QUESTIONS THAT HELP YOU ANALYZE SEQUENCE PARAGRAPHS

1. Is the order of events clear?
2. What time-order words or phrases does the writer use?
3. If the paragraph describes a task, are the instructions clear?
4. What did the writer do to keep your attention?
5. What steps did you think were not clear?
6. How could you make these steps or instructions clearer?

Underline three questions you will answer about the sequence paragraph. Write your answers here:

Answer ___: _____

_____

Answer ___: _____

_____

Answer ___: _____

_____

Name: _____ Date: _____

#2 Get Ready to Write: Sequence Paragraph

Directions

1. Choose a topic that involves a process—something that happens in stages or steps. Check the Idea Box for help.

2. Fill in the organizer with the steps for this process. Add boxes if necessary.

IDEA BOX

Explain how to . . .

get to school from your house

make a sandwich

succeed in school

play a game or sport

make a friend

impress your teacher

Your ideas:

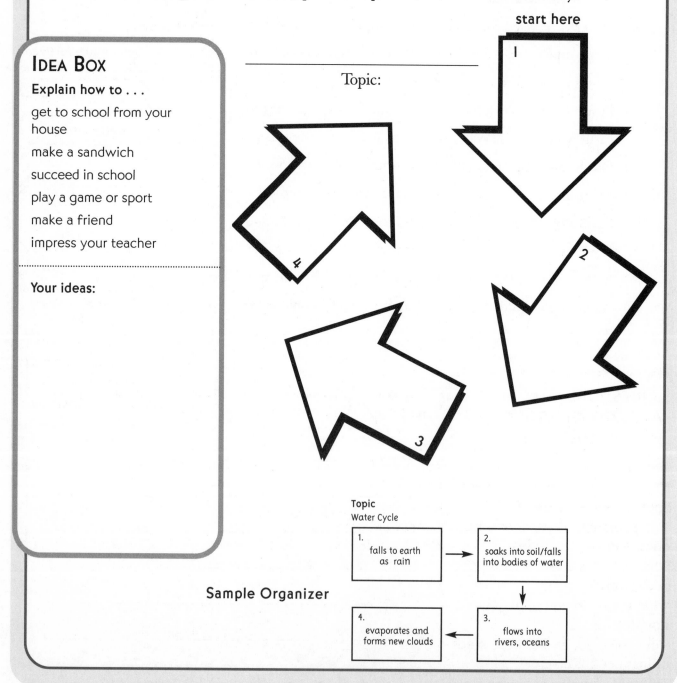

Topic: _____

start here

1

2

3

4

Topic
Water Cycle

| 1. falls to earth as rain | 2. soaks into soil/falls into bodies of water |

| 4. evaporates and forms new clouds | 3. flows into rivers, oceans |

Sample Organizer

Name: _____   Date: _____

#3 Write: Sequence Paragraph

Directions

1. Complete the writing plan below with ideas from your organizer (page #2).

2. Use the plan and the tip below to draft your paragraph.

3. Use the checklist to revise your writing.

Plan It Out

1. Possible leads:

- _____
  _____
  _____

- _____
  _____
  _____

2. Ideas for the conclusion:

- _____
  _____
  _____

- _____
  _____
  _____

3. Possible titles:

- _____

- _____

Write

Now you are ready to write your complete paragraph on lined paper.

SEQUENCE PARAGRAPH CHECKLIST

Content and Style

___ My title intrigues and focuses the reader.

___ The lead introduces the topic in an interesting, original way.

___ I've written clear steps in time order.

___ The conclusion helps the reader make sense of the paragraph.

___ I've used time-order words to organize the paragraph.

Mechanics

___ I've written in complete sentences and used end punctuation.

___ I've used capital letters properly.

Tip!
Does your sequence paragraph describe how to do something? Help make your steps and instructions clear by explaining them in detail and putting them in the correct order.

Expository Paragraph

An expository or informative paragraph shares information about a topic in a way that captures and maintains a reader's interest.

Introducing the Expository Paragraph

Provide student pairs with an assortment of expository written pieces (magazine articles, pamphlets from the doctor's office, encyclopedia articles) to examine, and ask them to explain what purpose these diverse pieces have in common. Answers may include that each piece of writing explains a topic or provides information to the reader. Follow up by asking students, *Which pieces did you find engaging or interesting Which were dull What techniques did writers use effectively to capture your attention*

Scaffolding Independent Writing

Post a chart in your room with questions that students can use to analyze expository paragraphs.

Questions That Help Students Analyze Expository Paragraphs
- What did I learn from this piece of writing?
- Is the topic clearly explained?
- Does the writer present and support a main idea?
- Is information presented logically?
- What parts could be clarified?
- What made the writing interesting?

Model for students how you read and respond to a clearly written expository paragraph. Then analyze the paragraph with students: Ask them to locate a lead with the main idea and decide whether it is effective; discuss the order in which facts and details are presented, and the author's purpose in doing so; and identify the conclusion and how it affects the reader.

After they have read a number of different expository pieces from magazine articles, newspaper stories, pamphlets, encyclopedia articles, and history texts, encourage students to use the questions above to analyze them. Ask students to come up with a list of the traits of a successful expository paragraph. The list might include: *the topic must be defined and narrow enough to be supported, each supporting statement must have a clear focus and relate directly to the topic,* and *the transition words or phrases help the reader follow along and reinforce the logic.*

Using the Independent Writing Activity Pages

Have students use the activity page set (pages 31–33) to practice writing their own expository paragraphs. Post the list of the traits of a strong expository paragraph and remind students of the questions they can use to evaluate their writing.

To finish up this lesson, have students discuss (in pairs, as a whole class, or in a one-on-one conference): *How do good nonfiction writers organize their information in expository writing How do they keep their readers' interest*

Name: _____   Date: _____

#1 Read and React: Expository Paragraph

Directions

1. Read the model paragraph.
2. Underline the descriptive words the author uses.
3. Choose two questions about the writing to answer.

Fire Up the Barbeque—It's December

Did you know that in Australia, January is a summer month?
Sounds strange to us North Americans, but it's true. You
probably know that Earth orbits the sun over the course of
the year. You may not know that Earth is actually tilted on its
axis as it orbits (picture Earth's "axis" as an imaginary pole
through the center of Earth). When the sun shines on the
Earth, its light spreads over the surface, but not evenly. The
portion of Earth tilted away from the sun gets less direct
sunlight. That hemisphere experiences less light and heat—in
other words, winter. Here in the northern hemisphere, that
time falls between October and March. In the southern
hemisphere, those are the summer months, because that is the
time of year that hemisphere receives the most light and heat
from the sun. As Earth continues on its orbit and reaches the
opposite side of the sun, the situation reverses. The northern
hemisphere is now tilted toward the sun, so it is summer here
and winter in the southern hemisphere. So if you're planning
a trip Down Under this Christmas, pack your swimsuit!

> The lead begins with a fascinating fact.

> The explanation begins with information that's familiar to the reader.

> A compare-and-contrast explanation helps the reader understand the concepts.

> The conclusion paints an entertaining picture to help the reader remember the information.

QUESTIONS THAT HELP YOU ANALYZE EXPOSITORY PARAGRAPHS

1. What did I learn from this piece of writing?
2. How well is the topic explained?
3. What main idea does the writing support?
4. How is the information presented?
5. What could be clarified?
6. What made the writing interesting?

Underline two questions you will answer about the
expository paragraph. Write your answers here:

Answer ___: _____

_____

Answer ___: _____

_____

#2 Get Ready to Write: Expository Paragraph

Directions

1. Choose a topic you know a lot about or would like to research. Check the Idea Box for help.

2. Fill in the organizer with the steps, stages, or major points you will use to help your reader understand the subject.

Point 1

Point 2

Point 3

Point 4

Main topic

IDEA BOX

how bees make honey

how hybrid cars work

how soccer has grown in popularity in the U.S.

what causes hiccups

why cheating hurts students

Your ideas:

Sample Organizer

Point 1
Earth is tilted on an axis—sometimes closer, sometimes farther from sun

Point 2
when one hemisphere is tilted closer, the other is farther from sun

Point 3
summer—hemisphere receives most light and heat from sun

Point 4
winter—hemisphere receives least light and heat from sun

Main topic:
What causes the northern and southern hemispheres to have opposite seasons?

Name: _____   Date: _____

#3 Write: Expository Paragraph

Directions

1. Complete the writing plan below with ideas from your organizer on page #2.

2. Use the plan and tip below to draft your paragraph.

3. Use the checklist to make sure you've included everything you need in your paragraph.

Plan It Out

1. Possible leads:

- _____
  _____
  _____

- _____
  _____
  _____

2. Ideas for the conclusion:

- _____
  _____
  _____

- _____
  _____
  _____

EXPOSITORY PARAGRAPH CHECKLIST

Content and Style

___ My title intrigues and focuses the reader.

___ My lead grabs the reader's attention and introduces the topic.

___ My explanation and descriptions are logical and clear.

___ The conclusion satisfies the reader.

___ I've chosen words carefully and used memorable images.

Mechanics

___ I've written in complete sentences and used end punctuation.

___ I've used capital letters properly.

Tip!
Specific nouns add spice to your writing. Have you used nouns that name things exactly, like *pit bull* instead of *dog*, or *cheddar* instead of just *cheese*?

3. Possible titles:

- _____

- _____

Write

Now you are ready to write your complete paragraph on lined paper.

Personal Essay

In a personal essay, a writer uses his or her own experience as the basis for a broader observation or commentary on life in general.

Introducing the Personal Essay

In preparation for this lesson, choose a story from your past to share with students. Once you've told them the story, ask students to discuss how they think the experience changed your perspective or what it taught you about life. Explain that this process of finding meaning in one's own life experience is the substance of a personal essay.

Scaffolding Independent Writing

Post a chart in your room with questions that students can use to analyze personal essays.

Questions That Help Students Analyze Personal Essays

- What is the essay's purpose?
- How does the author communicate the purpose?
- What part of the experience does the writer emphasize? How?
- How does the writer feel about the experience?
- How does the lead affect the reader? What information does it provide?
- How does the title relate to the essay?

Model for students how you read and respond to a personal essay, using the questions above to analyze a well-written example. Some good sources are in *Chicken Soup for the Preteen Soul* and other books in that series, as well as *Teaching Powerful Writing* by Bob Sizoo. Think aloud about what makes the essay effective. Then, have students read other essays independently. Encourage students to use the questions above to analyze essays after reading and to generate a list of traits of a good personal essay. The list might include: *a powerful lead, a clear purpose, memorable images,* and *descriptions of the writer's feelings and thoughts.*

Using the Independent Writing Activity Pages

Have students use the activity page set (pages 35–38) to practice writing their own personal essays. Post a list of the traits of effective personal essays and remind students of the questions they can use to evaluate the essays. You may also want to post these writing process tips:

1. Choose a memorable experience as the focus of your essay. Remember, if you don't care about it, your reader won't either.
2. Before you write, brainstorm about why this experience has meaning for you, and what you learned from it.
3. As you write, include details that will bring your description to life, and add details as more memories surface or ideas arise.
4. Engage your reader with dialogue, dramatic scenes, and suspense.

Encourage students to enrich their writing with sensory details and experiment with different ways of organizing their essays.

To finish up this lesson, ask students to discuss (in pairs, as a whole class, or in a one-on-one conference): *What do I think and feel about this piece*

Name: _____   Date: _____

#1 Read and React: Personal Essay

Directions

1. Read the model essay.
2. Choose two questions about the writing to answer.

Snow Day

On Thursday, I rushed to turn on the radio the moment I woke up. As the announcer droned through an endless list of school closings, I sat on the edge of the bed, crossed my fingers, and wished for school to be cancelled. When I'd almost given up hope, I heard an announcer say, "Ben Franklin–closed." A huge smile took over my face because I knew a rare day of fun and adventure awaited me.

I have loved snowy days ever since I was a little girl. As soon as I heard there was no school, I begged my older brother to go outside with me. Wrapped in many layers, we pitched snowballs, sculpted snowmen worthy of a museum, constructed forts until our fingers were stinging with numbness, and sledded down the neighbors' giant hill of a lawn. When we were too cold to stay outside any longer, we boiled water for hot cocoa and curled up on the couch. We snuggled into soft flannel pajamas and turned on the stereo. Our snowy afternoon ended with a deliciously long nap.

If you're lucky enough to get a snow day, make sure to go outside and take advantage of it. Someday, you and I might not even like the snow: perhaps we'll be too busy worrying about shoveling the driveway, making it to work, or paying the heating bill to enjoy the beauty and magic of a snowstorm. So on the next snow day, bundle up and let your winter adventures begin.

> The topic of this simple title is bound to interest school-going readers.

> The introduction begins with a memory the author loves.

> Great verbs paint a picture of the kids' actions.

> Sensory details make us feel what the experience is like.

> The conclusion sums up how the writer feels about the topic and invites a young reader to enjoy snow days while they last.

Questions that help you analyze personal essays

1. What is the essay's purpose?
2. How does the author communicate the purpose?
3. What part of the experience does the writer emphasize?
4. How does the writer feel about the experience?
5. How does the lead affect the reader?
6. How does the title relate to the essay?

Underline two questions you will answer about the personal essay. Write your answers on the back of this page.

#2 Get Ready to Write: Personal Essay

Directions

1. Choose a memory or experience that has special meaning for you. Check the Idea Box for help.

2. Fill in the organizer with memories, images, and sensory details to add to your essay.

Memories

Thoughts

Feelings

Topic

IDEA BOX

a terrifying experience when you were young

an important social event (wedding, sports) that you took part in

a family outing or vacation

a serious wrongdoing

something in your past you'd like to change

Your ideas:

How this experience changed my life:

_____

_____

_____

_____

Sample Organizer

Memories
listening to cancellations; hot cocoa; cozy pajamas; sledding; throwing snowballs

Thoughts
taking my time to appreciate this rare day

Feelings
hope, relief, excitement, cozy, comfortable feelings

How this experience changed my life: helped me realize how precious these playful, carefree times are when you're a kid; made me think that I should always take the time to enjoy them thoroughly

Topic
snow day memory

Name: _____   Date: _____

#3 Plan: The Personal Essay

Directions

Use your ideas from the organizer (page #2) to complete the writing plan below.

Plan It Out

1. Possible title:

_____

_____

> **Tip!**
> What would grab your reader's attention here?

2. Ideas for the introduction:

_____

_____

3. Most important memory to include:

_____

_____

4. Most important feeling to include:

_____

_____

5. Most important thought to include:

_____

_____

6. Ideas for the conclusion:

_____

_____

_____

> **Tip!**
> Think about how you want the reader to feel after reading your essay.

Name: _____   Date: _____

#4 Write: Personal Essay

Directions

1. Draft your essay on lined paper.

2. Use the questions below to revise your writing.

3. Use the checklist to make sure you've included everything you need in your personal essay.

Revise

Take some time to review your draft and revise. Here are some questions to ask about your draft:

- Is your lead engaging enough?

- Can you add or develop images to bring your memories to life for your reader?

- Does your title support your purpose?

- Have you made the reader feel a certain way at the end of your essay?

Two parts I can improve are (circle two): title, lead, feeling details, sensory details, memory details, conclusion.

Rewrites:

- _____
  _____
  _____
  _____
  _____

- _____
  _____
  _____
  _____
  _____

PERSONAL ESSAY CHECKLIST

Content and Style

___ I have a topic that interests me.

___ My title intrigues and focuses the reader.

___ My lead grabs the reader's attention and introduces the topic.

___ I've included clear, descriptive details that support my essay's purpose.

___ I've used transition words to help the reader follow my thoughts.

___ The conclusion makes the reader understand how I feel or think about the topic.

Persuasive Essay

A good persuasive essay convinces others to agree with your opinion.

Introducing the Persuasive Essay

Ask your students a provocative question that relates to their lives, for example: *o cell phones belong in school Should kids have obs during the summer* Allow a few minutes for several students to offer their opinions, and encourage the class to debate the issue respectfully. Then, ask students to reflect on their conversation: *id any of the volunteers say anything that reinforced or made you reconsider your own opinion*

Scaffolding Independent Writing

Post a chart in your room with questions that students can use to analyze persuasive essays.

Questions That Help Students Analyze Persuasive Essays
- What information does the lead provide?
- What is the essay's topic? Does the writer feel strongly about it?
- What is the writer's point of view?
- Does the writer support his or her arguments by using quotes? Predictions? Opposition points? Data? Comparisons?
- Are the arguments convincing or unconvincing? Why?
- How does the author address an opposing argument?

Model for students how you read and respond to a persuasive essay, using the questions above to analyze a well-written example. Good sources include the editorial section of a newspaper and the Scholastic magazine *Scope*. Think aloud about what makes the writing successful. Then have students read more essays independently and use the questions above to analyze them. Ask students to create a list of traits for a good persuasive essay. The list might include: *a clear topic, strong supporting arguments, facts, data, quotes, comparisons,* and *the fair presentation of an opposing argument.*

Using the Independent Writing Activity Pages

Have students use the activity page set (pages 40–43) to practice writing persuasive essays. Post the list of the traits of a strong persuasive essay and remind students of the questions they worked with to evaluate their own essays. Encourage students to rework arguments until they find the most persuasive points for their essay.

To finish up this lesson, ask students to discuss (in pairs, as a whole class, or in a one-on-one conference): *What is the purpose of a persuasive essay When might you use one*

A persuasive essay is meant to change the way a reader thinks. In order to write convincingly, the writer must choose a topic that genuinely interests him or her. Encourage students to write about something that touches, inspires, or even upsets them. Such a choice will ensure that students write in a voice that affects and persuades their readers.

Name: _____   Date: _____

#1 Read and React: Persuasive Essay

Directions

1. Read the model essay.

2. Choose two questions about the writing to answer.

Were the "Good Old Days" Really Better?

"When I was a kid, we spent our afternoons outdoors, not in front of the TV! When it rained, we read or played games–and I don't mean computer games. Kids today don't know how to do anything besides stare at a screen!" How many times have you heard adults talk like this?

Well, if you ask me, these statements are really unfair. First of all, most kids I know have at least two hours of homework a night, if not more. Second, like a lot of my friends, I am on a team–I play softball three times a week. Therefore, I get plenty of physical exercise and fresh air, and yes, more time away from the TV and computer! Adults always complain that kids don't read anymore. Maybe they have a point that kids don't read as much as they did before TV, but that doesn't mean we don't read. Do you think Harry Potter would be such a hit if kids didn't read anymore? In addition, when today's kids watch TV or do research on the Internet, we're learning about new people and places with better information than textbooks. When we use computers, we are learning skills we'll use all our lives.

Sure, some kids need less TV and more exercise and reading time. But many fifth graders like me already get plenty of both of these things–AND learn more. Just because life is different now than it was twenty-five or thirty years ago doesn't mean the "good old days" were better.

Underline two questions you will answer about the persuasive essay. Write your answers on the back of this page.

> This title engages the reader by asking a question.

> An opening quotation that sounds unfair sets the stage for the writer's argument.

> The author prepares the reader for a list of strong points.

> The writer acknowledges the other side.

> Then, he refutes the argument.

> The conclusion sums up major arguments.

> The last line leaves the reader with a new twist on a familiar phrase, and refers back to the title.

QUESTIONS THAT HELP YOU ANALYZE PERSUASIVE ESSAYS

1. How does the lead make the reader feel?
2. What is the essay's purpose? How can I tell?
3. How does the title help introduce the essay?
4. How does the writer feel about the topic?

Name: _____   Date: _____

#2 Get Ready to Write: Persuasive Essay

Directions

1. Choose a topic you feel strongly about. Check the idea box for help.

2. Fill in the organizer with your point of view and supporting points.

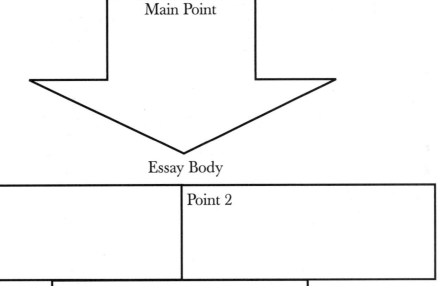

Main Point

Essay Body

Point 1	Point 2

Point 3

Opposing Argument

Counterargument

IDEA BOX

why school uniforms are or are not a good idea

whether locker searches are fair to students

the importance of computers in the classroom

whether community service should be included in the middle school curriculum

Your ideas:

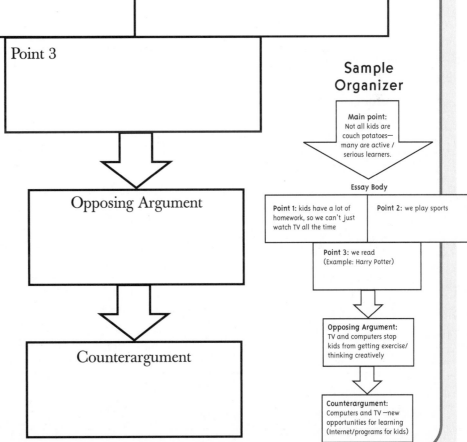

Sample Organizer

Main point: Not all kids are couch potatoes— many are active / serious learners.

Essay Body

Point 1: kids have a lot of homework, so we can't just watch TV all the time

Point 2: we play sports

Point 3: we read (Example: Harry Potter)

Opposing Argument: TV and computers stop kids from getting exercise/ thinking creatively

Counterargument: Computers and TV —new opportunities for learning (Internet/programs for kids)

#3 Plan: Persuasive Essay

Directions

Complete the writing plan below with ideas from your organizer (page #2).

Plan It Out

1. Possible leads (come up with at least two ideas):

- _____

  _____

- _____

  _____

2. Conclusion ideas:

- _____

  _____

- _____

  _____

3. Ideas for supporting your main point:

Point 1 _____

_____

Point 2 _____

_____

Point 3 _____

_____

> **Tip!**
> Which is your strongest point? Put it first or last to pack a punch.

Opposing argument and counterargument:

_____

_____

_____

_____

> **Tip!**
> Make sure to give facts or evidence as you refute (argue against) the opposing argument.

#4 Write: Persuasive Essay

Directions

1. Use the plan to draft your essay on lined paper.

2. Rewrite your essay using the revision tips below.

3. Use the checklist below to make sure you've included everything you need in your persuasive essay.

Revise

Check that your persuasive essay has support for each point. Here are five types of statements that can help convince your reader:

- Factual statements or statistics—show strong evidence (include your sources)
  Example: *Most kids I know have at least two hours of homework a night, if not more.*

- Value statements—show what something's worth
  Example: *Just because life is different now than it was twenty-five or thirty years ago doesn't mean the "good old days" were better.*

- Consequence statements—show the probable result of the decision or action
  Example: *When today's kids watch TV or do research on the Internet, we're learning about new people and places with better information than textbooks. When we use computers, we are learning skills we'll use all our lives.*

- Autobiographical Statements—show proof from the writer's personal experience
  Example: *Like a lot of my friends, I am on a team—I play softball three times a week. Therefore, I get plenty of physical exercise and fresh air, and yes, more time away from the TV and computer!*

- Quotes from others—show that other people agree with or against the position.
  Example: *"When I was a kid, we spent our afternoons outdoors, not in front of the TV! When it rained, we read or played games—and I don't mean computer games. Kids today don't know how to do anything besides stare at a screen!"*

Rewrite

Go back to your writing and add any changes.

PERSUASIVE ESSAY CHECKLIST

Content and Style

___ My title intrigues and focuses the reader.

___ The lead grabs the reader's attention and introduces the topic.

___ I have a clear topic and point of view.

___ I've included strong points that support my argument.

___ The opposing side of the argument is clear.

___ The conclusion will affect my reader the way I want it to.

Informative Essay

Purpose

To inform readers about a specific topic, or to clarify or explain a subject, process, or issue.

Introducing the Informative Essay

Ask students to think of a time they've been left in charge of something usually overseen by their parents or another adult in charge—making dinner, caring for a younger sibling, or taking public transportation alone, for example. How did the adults prepare them for the task? What resources helped students succeed independently? Did their parents provide tips, tools, examples, or sequenced instructions? Explain to students that the purpose of an informative essay is to *explain* a topic or *teach* a reader how to do something.

Scaffolding Independent Writing

Post a chart in your room with questions that students can use to analyze informative essays.

Questions That Help Students Analyze Informative Essays

- How does the lead work? What information does it provide?
- Has the essay's topic been clearly stated? What is it?
- What details support the topic?
- What did I learn from the information given?
- Does the writer use quotes? Predictions? Data? Comparisons? How do these elements help my understanding?
- How is the essay organized? (Where is the most important information presented?)

Model for students how you read and respond to an informative essay, using the questions above to analyze a well-written example. Search for interesting, well-written feature articles from science textbooks, newspapers, or magazines. Share one with the class and think aloud about what makes the essay good. Then, have students read two or three more essays on their own and encourage them to use the questions above to analyze them. Ask students to create a list of traits of a good informative essay. The list might include: *a clear topic, strong supporting details, facts, data, quotes,* and *lively writing.*

Using the Independent Writing Activity Pages

Have students use the activity page set (pages 45–49) to practice writing informative essays. Post a list of the traits of a strong informative essay and remind students of the questions they can use to evaluate the essays. Encourage students to figure out which points best support their essay writing and find the strongest, clearest points for their essay.

To finish up this lesson, ask students to discuss (in pairs, as a whole class, or in a one-on-one conference): *When would you find it useful to write an informative essay? When might you seek one out as a reader?*

#1 Read and React: Informative Essay

Directions

1. Read the model essay.

2. Choose three questions about the writing to answer.

Mom, Can We Get a Dog?

When I say I'm from a family of ten, people are usually surprised. I am quick to explain, however, that not all ten family members are people . . . only five of us are. But I consider our three dogs and two cats family members. Just like my parents, brothers, and me, they need food, shelter, medical care, and lots of love. Taking care of pets is a serious responsibility.

> The lead hooks the reader with a surprising statement.

> The final sentence makes the purpose of the essay clear.

If you're considering getting a pet, there's a lot you should know. Dogs, for example, need lots of exercise. Taking your dog to the park for a good run, a game of Frisbee, and some social time with other dogs is an important part of being a good dog owner. Cats, on the other hand, can be pretty happy staying indoors most of the time. They appreciate cozy spaces, simple toys like balls of yarn and fake mice, and lots of cuddling from people. If you let your cat outside, be sure it has a flea collar and a safe place to roam, far from the street. Both cats and dogs need to be fed healthy food on a regular schedule. It's also important to take them to the veterinarian for check-ups, or if you suspect they're not feeling well.

> This paragraph makes more specific points to explain what's behind the author's purpose.

"It's very important to spay or neuter your cat or dog," says Dr. Fine, our veterinarian. "Otherwise, you may wind up with unwanted puppies or kittens." Those unwanted animals often become strays, he explains, without families to care for them or enough food to eat. When the strays become older, they wind up having more puppies or kittens, and the problem continues. Spaying or neutering your pet is an important part of being a responsible pet owner.

> A quote from an expert encourages the reader to take the author's perspective seriously.

#1 Read and React: Informative Essay

(continued)

Adding pets to your family is great, but you should think carefully about whether you have the time and patience to take care of an animal for its whole life. Remember, you'll have to feed it, provide it with opportunities for exercise (if it's a dog), take it to the vet regularly, and have it spayed or neutered. If you're up to all that, though, then you're ready to be a pet owner! •——————

> The conclusion reiterates the main points of the essay and ends on an encouraging note.

QUESTIONS THAT HELP YOU ANALYZE INFORMATIVE ESSAYS

1. How does the lead work? What information does it provide?

2. Has the essay's topic been clearly stated? What is it?

3. What details support the topic?

4. What did I learn from the information given?

5. Does the writer use quotes? Predictions? Data? Comparisons? How do these elements help my understanding?

6. How is the essay organized? (Where is the most important information presented?)

Underline three questions you will answer about the informative essay. Write your answers here:

Answer ___: _____

_____

_____

_____

_____

Answer ___: _____

_____

_____

_____

_____

Answer ___: _____

_____

_____

_____

_____

#2 Get Ready to Write: Informative Essay

Directions

1. Choose a topic you can explain thoughtfully to a reader. Check the Idea Box for help.

2. Fill in the organizer with facts, ideas, statistics, and specific quotes that support your topic. Be sure to state your purpose for writing, too.

Topic:

Point 1:

Point 2:

Point 3:

Purpose:

IDEA BOX

how to: survive in middle school, play volleyball, be a great babysitter, or throw a surprise party

what makes a great bike

how too much sugar affects your body

Your ideas:

Sample Organizer

Topic:
owning a pet

Point 1:
pets need a lot of care.

Point 2:
different pets require different kinds of attention and care

Point 3:
you should spay or neuter your animal

Purpose:
to make readers think carefully about whether they are ready to be pet owners

#3 Plan: Informative Essay

Directions

Complete the writing plan below with ideas from your organizer (page #2).

Plan It Out

Record quotes, personal experiences, or statistical data to support each of the points.

	Fact	Quotes	Personal Experiences	Statistical Data
Point 1				
Point 2				
Point 3				

Other people or resources I might try: _____

_____

Name: _____ Date: _____

#4 Write: Informative Essay

Directions

1. Develop a strong lead and conclusion for your essay.

2. Use the plan from page #3 to draft your essay on lined paper. Include your favorite lead and the conclusion from below.

3. Use the checklist to make sure you've included all your ideas and polished the writing.

Lead and Conclusion

Try two different leads and see which works best.

Lead idea #1:

_____

_____

_____

_____

Lead idea #2:

_____

_____

_____

_____

Tip!
Consider using a question that makes the reader stop and think or a story with a conversational tone, like the one in the sample.

INFORMATIVE ESSAY CHECKLIST

Content and Style

___ My title intrigues and focuses the reader.

___ The lead grabs the reader's attention and introduces the topic.

___ I have a well-defined topic.

___ A reader will be able to follow my reasoning.

___ My purpose is clearly stated and supported throughout.

Write a conclusion that states your purpose:

_____

_____

_____

_____

Write

Now you are ready to write your complete essay on lined paper.

News Article

Purpose

A news story describes important or unusual events. Reporters gather facts from reliable sources, organize the information logically, and attempt to present the information from a neutral point of view.

Introducing the Informative Essay

Activate students' prior knowledge by asking if anyone in their homes reads the daily newspaper or online news articles. Ask: *What sorts of articles appear in the paper or online   Where do reporters get their information*

Post the parts of a news story in your classroom as a reference:

- Headline—catches the attention of the reader and presents the topic
- Byline—gives the writer credit
- Lead—tells the most important news
- Quote—gives importance and life to a story
- Body—answers the five W's: *who, what, when, where, why*
- End—leaves the reader with something memorable

Scaffolding Independent Writing

Post a chart in your room with questions to help analyze news stories.

Questions That Help Students Analyze News Articles

- What is the topic of the article?
- Does the title or headline provide the reader with a focus?
- How is the article structured? Where is the most important information?
- Are the sources reliable and authoritative?
- Is the story presented fairly? How so? How could it be fairer?
- Can I answer the *Who, What, Where, When,* and *Why* questions by examining the article?

Model for students how you read and respond to a news article, using the questions above to analyze a well-written example. Think aloud about what makes the news article effective. Next, have students read and compare two or three news articles, analyzing the articles with the questions above. Ask students to come up with a list of traits of a well-written news article. The list may include: *a clear and compelling headline, reliable sources, information presented from more than one perspective,* and *the five W's.*

To finish up this lesson, ask students to discuss (in pairs, as a whole class, or in a one-on-one conference): *In a well-written news article, what catches your interest and keeps you reading*

> **Tip!**
> You may want to point out that because of space limitations in printed formats, such as newspapers, an editor may cut the end of an article, lopping off the conclusion—this is what gives basic news articles a "cut-off" feel.

Name: _____   Date: _____

#1 Read and React: News Article

Directions

1. Read the model article.

2. Choose two questions about the writing to answer.

Springfield Schools Bursting at the Seams

Molly Whitaker spent Tuesday morning working at her teacher's desk. No, this wasn't a consequence of bad behavior or even a reward for a job well done; there was simply nowhere else for her to sit. Thanks to new housing and business construction in Springfield, a problem familiar to the nation's largest cities—overcrowded classrooms—has become the concern of Springfield residents.

> The lead begins with a memorable image and continues by presenting the basic focus of the article.

According to school board president Anita Fernandes, "Hollow Elementary has 750 students enrolled for this school year, yet the building was built for 550." What does that mean to students? It means classes are overcrowded: instead of 18 students per class, most have 32. There are not enough supplies to go around, not enough teachers, and not enough desks or classroom space. The school board approved the purchase of 10 trailers during last night's emergency budget meeting. This may ease some crowding this year, but all parties agree it is not a long-term solution.

> The details present all of the five W's.

The town, school board, and land developers have planned a meeting for Monday at 8 p.m. at Springfield High School. At that time, they will discuss the large class sizes for the coming year and what to do in the future. The public is welcome to attend.

> The conclusion points to future events about the issue and invites the reader to become involved.

QUESTIONS THAT HELP YOU ANALYZE NEWS ARTICLES

1. What is the topic of the article?

2. Does the title/headline provide the reader with a focus?

3. How is the article structured? Where is the most important information?

4. Are the sources reliable and authoritative?

5. Is the story presented fairly? How so? Or how could it be more fair?

6. Can I answer the *Who, What, Where, When,* and *Why* questions by examining the article?

Underline two questions you will answer about the news article. Write your answers on the back of this page.

Name: _____ Date: _____

#2 Get Ready to Write: News Article

Directions

1. Choose a topic to write about (pick a local issue that people are talking about—and that you care about—in your school or neighborhood). Check the Idea Box for help.

2. Do research and brainstorm details using the five W's to make sure your reader will understand the basic facts of the issue.

IDEA BOX

a natural event such as a flood, that affected your community

a local sports event

an issue regarding a major company or industry in your community

....

Your ideas:

Sample Organizer

Subject: Overcrowding in Springfield
Who? Kids in overcrowded schools
What? Classrooms are overcrowded; not enough supplies, rooms, teachers
Where? Springfield
When? Recent problem
Why? New construction and overpopulation
Quote from a knowledgeable source:
school board president

Subject: _____

Who? _____

What? _____

_____

_____

Where? _____

When? _____

Why? _____

_____

Quote from a knowledgeable source:

_____

_____

_____

_____

#3 Plan: News Article

Directions

1. Read the sample plan.

2. Using your own information from page #2, complete the planning organizer below.

3. Think of a headline that will draw a reader's attention to your article.

Plan It Out

Start with the most important details and end with the least important ones.

Lead

Most important details

Less important details

Least important details

Set a purpose

Sample Plan

Lead
Overcrowded classrooms are becoming a problem in this county.

Most Important details
750 kids in a school for 550, classrooms packed

Less important details
not enough supplies, rooms

Least important details
meeting open to the public

Set a purpose
Alert Springfield residents about a problem their kids face in schools

Headline ideas (think of at least two):

● _____

● _____

Name: _____ Date: _____

#4 Write: News Article

Directions

1. Draft your article on lined paper, following your plan (page #3).
2. Practice punctuating quotations and check that you've properly punctuated those in your draft.
3. Revise your article using the tips below and add your best headline (page #3).
4. Use the checklist to make sure you've included everything you need in your news article.

Using Quotes

Reporters often quote people word for word. Keep these rules in mind when using quotes:

- Place quotes around the speaker's words.
- Put punctuation *before* the closing quotation mark.
- Use a comma outside of the quote mark before beginning a quote.

Review the examples below, then add punctuation to the sample sentences.

Examples:

1. A member of the NASA crew said, "I know this shuttle is ready to fly!"
2. "We cannot change the schedule," the office manager said. "It will inconvenience too many other patients."

Sample sentences:

1. Only time will tell said Principal Vito whether school uniforms is a good idea
2. Ms. Grange responded I have concerns about it
3. Uniforms make getting ready for school easier commented one student
4. We've had great success remarked the Uniforms R-Us spokesperson. Most parents prefer not to buy so many new clothes.

Revise

Add any details that will help make your article strong and clear.

> **Tip!**
> **Ideas for Revising a News Article**
> Ask yourself these questions to make your article clearer:
> - Did I include the five W's?
> - Is my viewpoint clear?
> - Is the evidence convincing?
> - Did I use reliable sources?

> ## NEWS ARTICLE CHECKLIST:
> **Content and Style**
> ___ I've written a short, attention-grabbing headline.
> ___ My lead makes clear all basic facts and the purpose of my article.
> ___ The essential details come first.
> ___ The article includes the five W's.
> ___ The article presents a reliable source for information.
> **Mechanics**
> ___ I've used quotation marks correctly.

CHAPTER 3

Writing Fiction

In order to help students become effective writers, we must help them become good readers first. By deciphering what successful authors have done before them, students can make informed, purposeful choices in their own writing. For this reason, before I have students write any fiction, we spend time "reading as writers." We delve into texts, lines, and words looking for subtle clues and "tricks of the trade." I often find that students get so excited by their discoveries about the writing they read that they are ready to jump into writing their own stories.

Keep in mind that there will always be students who resist fiction writing, and this is okay, too. Not everyone has the passion to make up stories. However, remind these students that you are not asking them to be the next Cynthia Rylant or Walter Dean Meyers. You are just asking them to be the most competent writers that they can be—and learning how to write a story is part of their journey.

Use the following organizers and strategy sheets to support students as they become independent fiction writers. Students can use each set of activity pages multiple times as they work on different fiction writing assignments. These lessons help students step through the different stages of the writing process and encourage them to think critically about their own writing.

To help students, create a poster with these tips to hang in your room:

- Prewrite: Take time to search for and collect ideas. Look for interesting sensory descriptions, compelling thoughts, or exciting events.

- Write: Form your ideas into a draft. Concentrate on collecting great phrases, words, and ideas that focus on your topic.

- Revise: Keep working on your writing until you feel that every word, phrase, and line says what it is meant to say.

> ### Lessons in This Section
>
> **Paragraphs**
> - Narrative
> - Character Sketch
> - Setting a Scene
> - Building a Plot
> - Developing a Theme
>
> **Longer Formats**
> - Short, Short Story
> - Fable

Narrative Paragraph

Narrative paragraphs tell a story with specific details about events and people. They can contain snippets of a conversation, describe a person or a setting, or share a person's inner thoughts.

Introducing the Narrative Paragraph

Have students start gathering ideas for narrative paragraphs by writing in a journal or a log and making lists of interesting experiences and people. To get students brainstorming, pose these questions: *Who are memorable people or characters in your life What places interest you What kinds of adventures do you like to take or read about What do you NOT like to do*

Scaffolding Independent Writing

Post a chart in your room with questions that students can use to analyze narrative paragraphs.

Questions That Help Students Analyze Narrative Paragraphs

- What is the author's purpose?
- What details support this purpose?
- How does the author organize ideas?
- Did the author use figurative language: metaphors, similes, personification, and alliteration? How did it add to the paragraph?
- How could this paragraph be improved?
- What "showing" details improved the paragraph?

Model for students how you read and respond to a short narrative, using the questions above to analyze a well-written example. Think aloud about what makes the narrative effective and well written. After students have read a number of different narrative paragraphs, encourage them to use the questions above to analyze the paragraphs. Ask students to come up with a list of traits for a strong narrative paragraph. The list might include: *describes clearly what a person or character does, tells a story, has a clear point of view, uses sensory details,* and *creates a mood.*

Using the Independent Writing Activity Pages

Have students use the activity page set (pages 57–59) to practice writing their own narrative paragraphs. Post the list of the traits of a strong narrative paragraph and remind students of the questions they worked with to evaluate the paragraphs. Help students sequence the events in their paragraph by having them practice writing the order of simple events, such as getting ready for school or making lunch. Also, encourage students to continue to brainstorm "showing" details because readers should be able to see, hear, touch, taste, and feel what they have written.

To finish up this lesson, ask students to discuss (in pairs, as a whole class, or in a one-on-one conference): *What do I enjoy most about my favorite stories What do I want to try in my next narrative paragraph*

Name: _____   Date: _____

#1 Read and React: Narrative Paragraph

Directions

1. Read the model paragraph.

2. Choose three questions about the writing to answer.

Skunk Motel •————————————————————————

The skunks can live under our porch, as long as they are quiet
and never spray. If they come out on a summer night and spray
their bitter scent in our yard—everything changes. "We can't be
a motel for the neighborhood!" Mom says, digging out the
safe-trap from the hall closet. Over many summers, Mom has
become a pro skunk catcher. She sneaks open the screen door
and plants the trap—an open cage with peanut butter inside. She
closes the screen door and waits and watches. Then, clang! The
cage door closes and the stunned skunk peers up at Mom. She
tosses the cage in the back of her truck and drives five miles out
of town to a wooded area. There, she relocates the skunk. •

> The title adds humor to the story.

> This lead raises the question: What might happen if the skunks are noisy and smelly?

> The quote shows how Mom really felt about the skunks.

> The scene is funny—it paints Mom as a detective cornering a suspect.

> A sequence of events ends with a concluding action that wraps up the story.

QUESTIONS THAT HELP YOU ANALYZE NARRATIVE PARAGRAPHS

1. What is the author's purpose?

2. What details support this purpose?

3. How does the author organize ideas?

4. Did the author use figurative language: metaphors, similes, personification, and alliteration? How did it add to the paragraph?

5. How could this paragraph be improved?

6. What "showing" details improved the paragraph?

Underline three questions you will answer about the narrative paragraph. Write your answers here:

Answer ___: _____

_____

Answer ___: _____

_____

Answer ___: _____

_____

Name: _____ Date: _____

#2 Get Ready to Write: Narrative Paragraph

Directions

1. Choose a story idea you'll enjoy writing about. If you need an idea, check the Idea Box.

2. Using the organizer, brainstorm the events that happen in your story.

3. Organize the events in the order in which they occurred.

IDEA BOX

The time my sister and I

_____

a skateboarding adventure

hamster trouble

a bout of stage fright

last week's big mistake

the best Friday night

Your ideas:

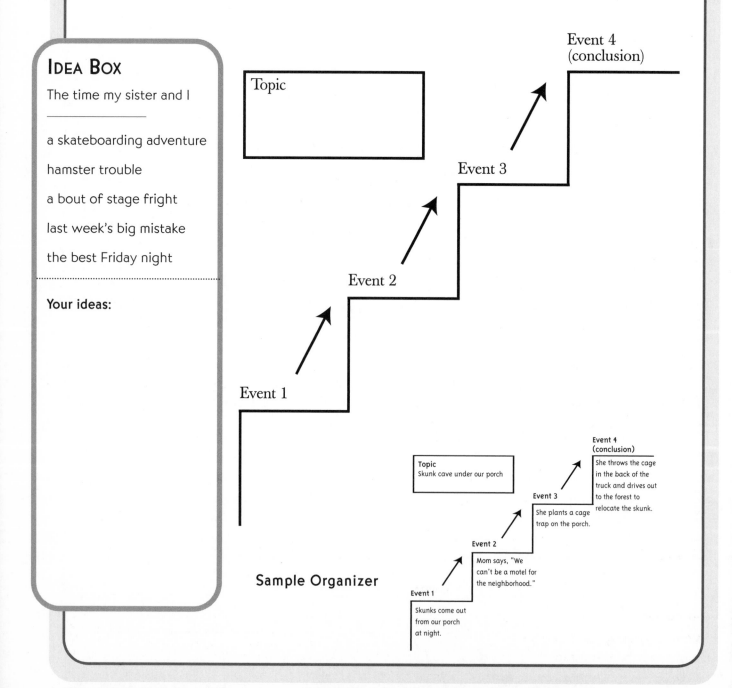

Topic

Event 4
(conclusion)

Event 3

Event 2

Event 1

Sample Organizer

Topic
Skunk cave under our porch

Event 1
Skunks come out from our porch at night.

Event 2
Mom says, "We can't be a motel for the neighborhood."

Event 3
She plants a cage trap on the porch.

Event 4
(conclusion)
She throws the cage in the back of the truck and drives out to the forest to relocate the skunk.

Name: _____   Date: _____

#3 Write: Narrative Paragraph

Directions

1. Write a plan for your narrative paragraph using the ideas from your organizer (page #2).
2. Use the plan to write a first draft on lined paper.
3. Revise your paragraph using the tips below. Then write out a final draft.
4. Use the checklist to make sure you've included all your ideas and polished the writing.

Plan It Out

Specific descriptions you can use for each event:

Event 1 _____

Event 2 _____

Event 3 _____

Event 4 _____

Write

Use the best ideas you came up with in your organizer to write a first draft on lined paper.

Tip! Strengthening a Narrative Paragraph

Sample description sentence:

Skunks come out on our porch at night.

Sample description sentence revised:

As the sun disappeared behind the trees, I could hear the pitter-patter of skunk paws tiptoeing across our flagstone porch.

Think: How did the revised sentence add to the description? Instead of telling about what the skunks did, the revised sentence shows us the setting and how the skunks moved—the sun "disappears" and the skunks "tiptoe" instead of "come out." Sensory words like *pitter-patter* also help paint the picture.

Revise

Add show-don't-tell details to make your writing stronger.

NARRATIVE PARAGRAPH CHECKLIST

Content and Style

____ I've written a short, snappy title.

____ The lead grabs the reader's attention and introduces the topic.

____ I've written clear, descriptive events, told in time order.

____ I've included show-don't-tell descriptions.

____ The conclusion makes the reader understand how I got from the first event to the last.

Character Sketch

A character sketch is a short piece of writing that shows something important about a person or a character. It is a building block of a good story.

Introducing the Narrative Paragraph

Explain to students that understanding characters is a key to understanding and enjoying the stories they read. Ask students to share favorite characters from stories or movies. Discuss what made those characters memorable. Answers may include: *details about the characters' actions, what they said,* and *how they looked at life.*

Scaffolding Independent Writing

Post a chart in your room with questions students can use to analyze character sketches.

Questions That Help Students Analyze Character Sketches

- What does the character look like?
- What does the character do?
- What does the character say?
- What does the character think or feel?
- What do others say about the character?

Model for students how you read and respond to a character sketch, using the questions above. Some good examples of writing similar to a character sketch include the short biographical articles about celebrities and sports stars that appear in magazines like *Seventeen* or *Sports Illustrated.* Other models include author bios on book covers. Allow time for students to read several character sketches on their own and use the questions above to analyze the writing.

Using the Independent Writing Activity Pages

Have students use the activity page set (pages 61–63) to practice writing their own character sketch about a favorite character from a book. Brainstorm with students a running list of words that describe a character's personality—*stubborn, talented, athletic,* and so on. Leave the list hanging in the room so students can add traits as they think of them. Encourage students to strive for descriptions that go beyond the physical and include the way characters think, act, and feel—as well as how others react to the character. Post a list of traits for a sharp character sketch and remind students of the questions they worked with to evaluate character sketches.

To finish up this lesson, ask students to discuss (in small groups, pairs, or in a one-on-one conference): *Do I know my character well enough to write about him or her in a new situation How does he or she usually behave Does or will my character change*

> **Tip!**
> When they first describe a character they've created, it is often helpful for students to work from a visual aid. I cut out many different faces of "characters" from magazines and allow students to choose one that interests them. Then, the students create a "life" for the chosen character. Hint: stay away from famous people or advertisements that provide information about the person.

Name: _____ Date: _____

#1 Read and React: Character Sketch

Directions

1. Read the model character sketch.

2. Choose three questions to answer about the writing.

Character Sketch for Timothy From *The Cay*
by Theodore Taylor

Timothy is an older man from the West Indies. He is not

the easiest person to get along with but he is a protector.

When he was stranded on the raft with Phillip, an eleven-

year-old boy from Virginia, he would not hand out the water.

Instead, he locked it up saying that they may need the water

for later. Phillip thinks Timothy is stubborn. He even

says that he begins to dislike him. But Timothy's actions

show that he has good survival skills.

> These descriptions show what the character says and does.

> Here we see what others say about the character.

> The last sentence wraps things up by drawing a conclusion about the character.

QUESTIONS THAT HELP YOU ANALYZE CHARACTER SKETCHES

1. What does the character look like?
2. What does the character do?
3. What does the character say?
4. What does the character think or feel?
5. What do others say about the character?

Underline three questions you will answer about the character sketch. Write your answers here:

Answer ___: _____

_____

Answer ___: _____

_____

Answer ___: _____

_____

Name: _____   Date: _____

#2 Get Ready to Write: Character Sketch

Directions

1. Choose a favorite character from a story or book that you have read.
2. Brainstorm ideas and details about the character, using the organizer below.
3. Choose two or three tips for writing about a character to help make your sketch shine.

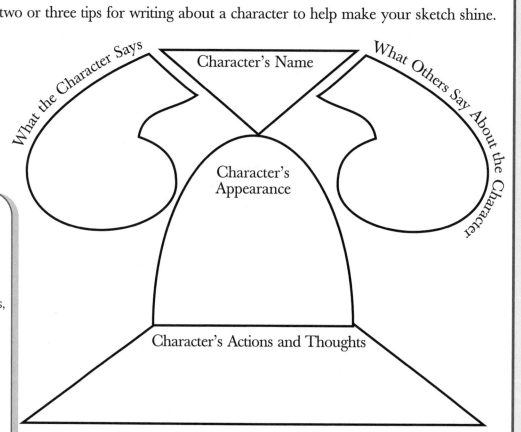

Tip!

A writer shows what a character is like by

- describing the character's physical appearance
- showing the character's speech, thoughts, feelings, actions
- showing how he or she interacts with other characters
- using powerful, exact adjectives that accurately describe what you want the reader to see (stay clear of words that don't say much about the character, such as *nice* and *good*)

Draw a conclusion: This character is a _____ kind of person because _____

_____ .

Sample Organizer

Draw a conclusion: This character is a <u>persevering</u> kind of person because <u>he</u> <u>does what he has to do to survive—even if</u> <u>it means not making friends.</u>

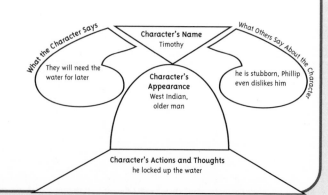

Graphic Organizers and Strategy Sheets That Scaffold Writing From Paragraphs to Essays • Scholastic Teaching Resources

Name: _____   Date: _____

#3 Write: Character Sketch

Directions

1. Write a plan for your character sketch using ideas from your organizer (page #2).
2. Use the plan to write a first draft on lined paper.
3. Revise your paragraph, using the tips below. Then write out a final draft.
4. Use the checklist to make sure you've included all your ideas and polished the writing.

Plan It Out

How do you feel about the character? _____

_____

What really makes this character tick? What do you want readers to understand about

this character?_____

_____

Write

Use the best ideas you came up with in your organizer to write a first draft on lined paper.

Strengthening a Character Sketch

 Sample character trait sentence:

Timothy was cautious.

Sample character trait sentence revised:

When he was on the raft with Phillip, he would not hand out the water. Instead, he locked it up saying that they may need the water for later.

Think: How did the revised sentence add to the writing? Instead of telling about the kind of person Timothy is, the writer reveals that he is cautious by showing his actions: saving the water for later.

Revise

Can you add any actions that show your character's personality? Adding these details will make your sketch stronger. Revise your writing on lined paper.

CHARACTER SKETCH CHECKLIST

Content and Style

___ I've included an example of the character's actions, feelings, and thoughts.

___ I've included an example of what others think or feel about the character.

___ I've used either an anecdote, question, or quote.

___ The reader can pick out a clear trait for this character.

___ I've included strong descriptions with powerful adjectives.

Mechanics

___ I've used a period, question mark, or exclamation point to end each complete sentence.

Setting a Scene

The setting is the time and place in which the action of a story occurs. Writers include environmental elements, such as stormy weather or rocky terrain, and time details, such as the setting sun, falling snowflakes, and even historical elements, such as a covered wagon, to help set the tone and historical context for the story.

Introducing the Setting

Explain to students that understanding a story's setting helps them better understand the stories they read. It will also help them build an appropriate and interesting setting for the characters and plot events in their own stories. Ask students to describe the setting of the classroom: What important time and place elements might give a reader hints that a story is taking place in a classroom? Then discuss what makes settings memorable or important in a story. Answers may include: *sensory details*, *details about mood*, and *changes in the setting*.

Scaffolding Independent Writing

Post a chart in your room with questions students can use to analyze settings.

Questions That Help Students Analyze Settings

- What is the time of day, day of the week, month, season, and year?
- What are the weather conditions?
- Are there any place names?
- What is the mood of the place?
- How does the character behave in this setting?
- How is this setting important to the character(s) and the action?

Model for students how you identify and respond to a story's setting, using the questions above. Some good examples of setting descriptions appear in the travel section of a newspaper or in travel and leisure magazines. You can also pick up a few pamphlets at a travel agency. Discuss what the writers include in order to make their setting inviting. Allow time for students to read descriptions of a number of settings and encourage them to use the questions above to analyze the writing.

Using the Independent Writing Activity Pages

Have students use the activity page set (pages 65–67) to practice writing their own vivid settings. Post a list of traits for a solid setting and remind students of the questions they worked with to evaluate settings. Encourage students to strive for descriptions that show the five senses. You may find that having them sketch the setting they've created and then make written notes about it gives them a clearer picture for their writing.

To finish up this lesson, have students discuss (in pairs, as a whole class, or in a one-on-one conference): *How can adding details about setting improve my stories*

> **Tip!**
> When I teach students to describe a setting, I use the same strategy that I use with character sketches since it often helps students to work from a visual aid. I cut out many different pictures of places from magazines. I allow students to choose the setting that interests them. Then, the students create a place for these images. (Hint: stay away from pictures with people in them—students may become sidetracked by the characters and lose their focus on time and environmental details.)

#1 Read and React: Setting

Directions

1. Read the model setting-sketch.

2. Choose three questions to answer about the sketch.

Beach Scene

The August sun blazed down from a toothpaste-blue sky at Jones Beach. The tiny grains of sand heated up like hot coals under the boy's feet. All around he could hear the sound of the waves crashing up against the shore. It was a constant hum. His tongue tickled with the bitter saltwater spray. But he was whistling. What could be wrong with a day spent tossing a beach ball as smooth as a new car? He jumped, skipped, and tossed the beach ball high into the air. Never before had he felt so free.

> Sensory details about the weather and sky appeal to feeling, taste, sound, and sight.

> Whistling is a detail that shows happiness.

> The closing shows how this ideal setting makes the boy feel joyous.

QUESTIONS THAT HELP YOU ANALYZE SETTINGS

1. What is the time of day, day of the week, month, season, and year?

2. What are the weather conditions?

3. Are there any place names?

4. What is the mood of the place?

5. How does the character behave in this setting?

6. How is this setting important to the characters and the action?

Underline three questions you will answer about the setting paragraph. Write your answers here:

Answer ___: _____

_____

Answer ___: _____

_____

Answer ___: _____

_____

#2 Get Ready to Write: Setting

Directions

1. Find a picture of a person in an interesting setting.

2. Brainstorm descriptive details about the setting and imagine how the setting helps, hurts, or changes the person. Fill in the organizer.

3. Use the tips in the box to make your description of the setting strong.

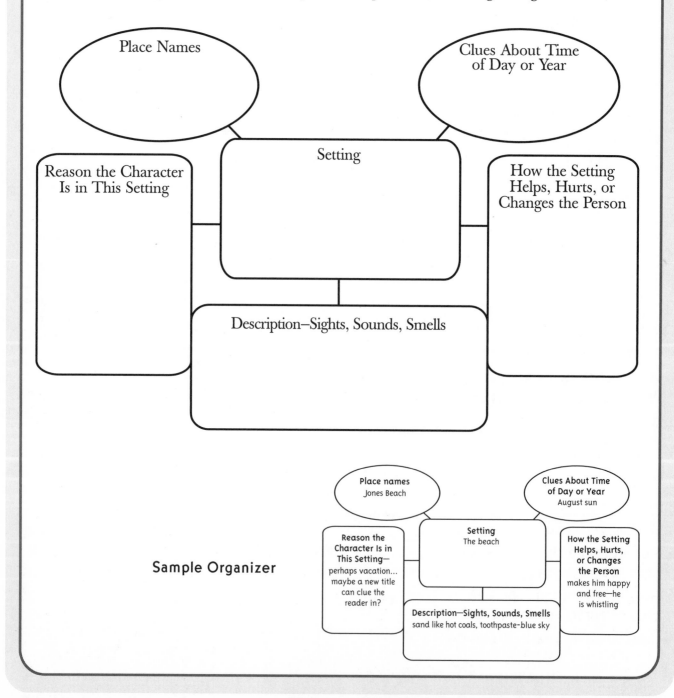

Place Names

Clues About Time of Day or Year

Reason the Character Is in This Setting

Setting

How the Setting Helps, Hurts, or Changes the Person

Description—Sights, Sounds, Smells

Sample Organizer

Place names — Jones Beach

Clues About Time of Day or Year — August sun

Reason the Character Is in This Setting— perhaps vacation... maybe a new title can clue the reader in?

Setting — The beach

How the Setting Helps, Hurts, or Changes the Person — makes him happy and free—he is whistling

Description—Sights, Sounds, Smells — sand like hot coals, toothpaste-blue sky

#3 Write: Setting

Directions

1. Write a plan for your setting paragraph using your organizer (page #2).
2. Use your plan to draft your paragraph on lined paper.
3. Revise your paragraph, using the tips below. Then write out a final draft.
4. Use the checklist to make sure you've included all your ideas and polished the writing.

Plan It Out

The mood you want to show in your description is _____

The most important setting description is _____

_____

Other setting descriptions you want to add: _____

_____

How does this setting change, help, or make problems for your character(s)? _____

_____

Write

Use the best ideas you came up with in your organizer to write a first draft.

Tip! Strengthening a Setting Paragraph

Sample descriptive sentence:

The sand was hot on the boy's feet.

Sample descriptive sentence revised:

The tiny grains of sand heated up like hot coals under the boy's feet.

Think: How did the revised sentence add to the writing? Instead of "telling" us the sand was hot, the writer revealed (or let us draw our own conclusions) by describing it as "hot coals." The description of the "tiny grains" also makes you see the sand and feel its graininess between your toes!

Revise

Can you add any details to make your setting stronger? Revise your writing on lined paper.

SETTING CHECKLIST

Content and Style

____ I've included sensory details.

____ I've included place names and the season or time.

____ I've shown how this setting changes, helps, or makes problems for the person.

Mechanics

____ I've used commas in a series.

____ I've used a period, question mark, or exclamation point to end each complete sentence.

Building a Plot

Plot is the action or sequence of events in a story. There are five basic elements in a plot that "move" the story along: exposition (establishes the conflict), rising action (events around the conflict that build toward a turning point), climax (turning point), falling action (resulting events), and denouement (resolution of the conflict). In their own fiction writing, students need to include the story's big problem (conflict), several events that build toward a turning point, the climax, and a resolution.

Introducing Plot

Explain to students that understanding plot will help them learn how stories are put together successfully. Discuss what makes plots memorable or important in movies students have seen or in stories they've read. Answers may include: *good build-up, suspense, realistic character actions and conflicts,* and *unexpected or satisfying solutions to problems.*

Scaffolding Independent Writing

Post a chart in your room with questions students can use to analyze plots.

Questions That Help Students Analyze Plot

- What outside conflicts (setting, characters, objects) affect the main character?
- What conflicts does the main character have with him or herself?
- How does the writer build suspense?
- Are there any twists, surprises, or reversals in the plot?
- How is the story's main problem resolved?

Read aloud a picture book with a strong, plot-driven focus, like *Freedom on the Menu* by Carole Boston Weatherford. Model for students how you read and respond to a plot, using the questions above. Choose several more plot-driven stories for students to read on their own. Discuss what the writers include in order to make their plot complete. Post a large picture of a plot line in your room.

PLOT POINT DIAGRAM

Climax

Rising Action

Plot Point 2
(Falling Action)

Plot Point 1
(Exposition)

Denouement

When you read different stories aloud, you can tack up cards that correspond to each part in each story. Then, allow time for students to read a number of short plots. After they have read a number of stories for plot, encourage students to use the questions above to analyze them.

Using the Independent Writing Activity Pages

Have students use the activity page set (pages 69–71) to practice writing their own polished plot. Post a list of traits for a well-constructed plot and remind students of the questions they can use to evaluate plots. Encourage students to invite a peer to read their plot—a fresh set of eyes can reveal where a storyline becomes unclear.

To finish up this lesson, have students discuss (in pairs, as a whole class, or in a one-on-one conference): *What in a plot sparks my interest or curiosity What about a particular resolution worked the best*

Tip!
You can teach plot development with comic strips. They have a short-story format in which the illustrator describes the setting and characters and the writer completes the plot outline by the final frame. Students can work in pairs to deconstruct the comic-strip plots. (Hint: the resolution in comics is often an expression on a character's face or just one word.)

Name: _____   Date: _____

#1 Read and React: Plot

Directions

1. Read the model story.

2. Choose three questions to answer about the writing.

A Stray Night

It was early fall. A pumpkin smiled on the back porch of a white Victorian house. Anne Marie sat on the porch with Buddy, a stray cat. The morning dew glistened and Anne Marie's glasses fogged up with dew. Her braids were still wet from her shower. Buddy tried to swat them, and she giggled. Anne Marie loved playing with her outside cat. The only sounds that Saturday morning were the paperboy's bike brakes screeching to a stop at each gate. And, then there was the ping of dry cat food in the dish. Anne Marie was just eight and her father said that if she wanted this cat, she could keep him—outside. But she'd have to care for him. So Anne Marie set him up a box to sleep in and gave him food. He'd stayed for two days.

> The setting and characters are introduced with sensory details to paint a picture of the scene.

> The final sentence of the first paragraph provides the first event in the plot.

Later, when Anne Marie called Buddy for supper, he did not come. She looked all over the yard, the block, the neighborhood. Where could he be? Anne Marie sat by the screen door on the porch until her father told her it was too chilly and she needed to close it. That night Anne Marie did not sleep much, thinking about all the things that can happen at night to a small grey cat.

> The problem is revealed.

> The second event in the plot occurs.

In the morning, as Anne Marie poured her cereal she heard a familiar meow. It was Buddy, clawing at the screen for breakfast. Anne Marie jumped up, spilling her orange juice, and raced out onto the porch. She scooped up Buddy into her arms. He wiggled out and curled up in his box. Anne Marie thought, *He has a mind of his own!* And, she would have sworn she saw a smile on his little cat mouth.

> This event marks the turning point—the time when things change in the story.

> The concluding sentence provides resolution to the story.

QUESTIONS THAT HELP YOU ANALYZE PLOT

1. What outside conflicts (setting, characters, objects) affect the main character?

2. What conflicts does the main character have with him- or herself?

3. How does the writer build suspense?

4. Are there any twists, surprises, or reversals in the plot?

5. How is the story's main problem resolved?

Underline three questions you will answer about the story. Write your answers on the back of this page.

#2 Get Ready to Write: Plot

Directions

1. Read over the model plan and then choose a story from your life you want to write about.

2. Brainstorm notes about the setting, characters, what happened first in the story, the turning point, and the main problem and its resolution. Fill in the organizer.

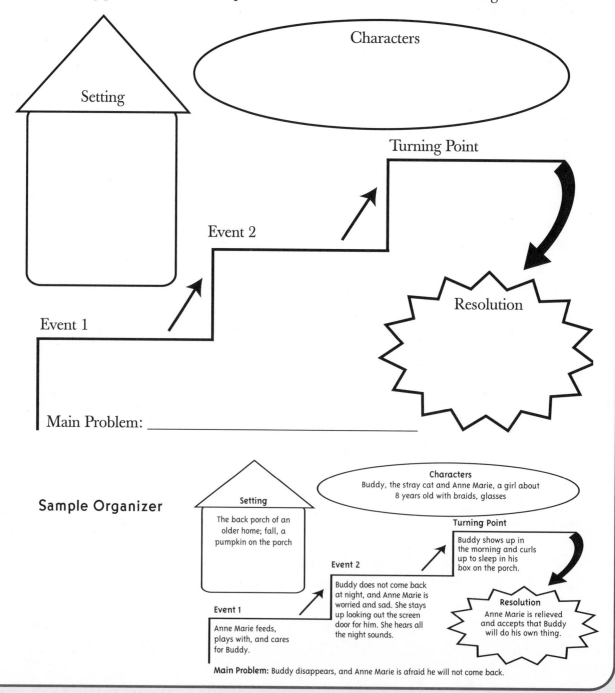

Sample Organizer

Setting
The back porch of an older home; fall, a pumpkin on the porch

Characters
Buddy, the stray cat and Anne Marie, a girl about 8 years old with braids, glasses

Turning Point
Buddy shows up in the morning and curls up to sleep in his box on the porch.

Event 2
Buddy does not come back at night, and Anne Marie is worried and sad. She stays up looking out the screen door for him. She hears all the night sounds.

Event 1
Anne Marie feeds, plays with, and cares for Buddy.

Resolution
Anne Marie is relieved and accepts that Buddy will do his own thing.

Main Problem: Buddy disappears, and Anne Marie is afraid he will not come back.

Name: _____   Date: _____

#3 Write: Plot

Directions

1. Write a plan for your story using your plot organizer (page #2).
2. Use your plan to draft your story
3. Revise your story using the tips below. Then write out a final draft.
4. Use the checklist to make sure you've included all your ideas and polished the writing.

Plan It Out

What is an important detail about the setting of your story? _____

_____

What event starts off the plot—is this the best way to begin? _____

_____

What is another possible way you could end the story and solve the problem? _____

_____

How does this setting change, help, or make problems for your character(s)? _____

_____

Write

Use the best ideas you've come up with to write a first draft on lined paper.

(Tip!) Strengthening a Story's Plot

Sample plot sentence:
Anne Marie looked for the cat.

Sample plot sentence revised:
Later, when Anne Marie called Buddy for supper, he did not come.

Think: How did the revised sentence add to the writing? This sentence indicates the time order of events with the word *Later*. It also shows a cause-and-effect relationship—she called for the cat (cause); he did not come (effect).

Tip: Some other time-order words that show how the action moves include: *one day, first, then, later,* and *all of a sudden.*

Revise

Can you add any details to make your plot stronger? Revise your writing on lined paper.

PLOT CHECKLIST

Content and Style

___ My story has a beginning, a middle, and an end.

___ There is a clear problem that is resolved.

___ I've included setting and characters.

___ I've used time-order words.

Mechanics

___ I used a period, question mark, or exclamation point to end each complete sentence.

Developing a Theme

Theme is a tricky concept for most students. It is the statement about life that the story is trying to make—sometimes we call it "the big idea" of the story.

Introducing Theme

Explain to students that understanding theme will help them better understand a writer's big idea or message. In fact, often there are several big ideas in a story and two readers may understand the theme of the same story differently. Both readers' points of view are valid if each can be supported with evidence from the story. Ask students to define *theme* in their own words. Answers may include: *the author's message, the point of the story, an important idea.* Write several theme statements on the board, such as: *childhood is the best time of life, friends are loyal to the end,* and *growing up is not easy,* and discuss why these are themes and not plots.

Scaffolding Independent Writing

Post a chart in your room with questions students can use to analyze theme.

Questions That Help Students Analyze Theme

- What is the big idea or ideas?
- What do the characters do or say about the big idea?
- What is the writer's point or message?
- What can the theme tell you about life?

Accessible and strong themes can be found in different fairy tales or fables. For older students, you may want to choose a nontraditional or "fractured" fairy tale, like Robert Munsch's *The Paper Bag Princess,* which turns a traditional fairy-tale relationship on its head. Model for students how you read and respond to a fairy tale's theme, using the questions above. Discuss what the author includes in order to emphasize the theme. Point out that the theme is often revealed through repeated words or phrases, symbols, important plot events, dialogue, or changes in characters' actions, thoughts, and feelings. Allow time for students to read a number of short stories for theme and use the questions above to analyze the writing.

> **Tip!**
> Brainstorm a list of common theme topics with students. Get them started with some of these: *childhood, death, courage, family, friendship, growing up, hate, hope, identity, justice, love, patience, prejudice, success, trust, truth, unhappiness, violence.*

Using the Independent Writing Activity Pages

Have students use the activity page set (pages 73–75) to practice writing their own authentic theme. Post a list of traits for "big ideas" and remind students of the questions they worked with to evaluate theme. Encourage students to allow another student to read a draft of their story and state the theme in his or her own words. If the theme is very different from what the writer intended, this is a time to return to the story and find points to emphasize.

To finish up this lesson, have students discuss (in pairs, as a whole class, or in a one-on-one conference): *What about the way a particular theme I developed worked the best* Help them restate, in their own words, what the theme is.

Name: _____   Date: _____

#1 Read and React: Theme

Directions

1. Read the model.
2. Choose three questions about the writing to answer.

Androclese and the Lion (a retelling of a Greek fable)

Androclese, a young man with little money but a kind spirit, was a prisoner of a cold-hearted king who wanted him to serve as a gladiator for his entertainment. On the day of the circus, Androclese was thrown to the lions with only a spear to protect himself. The king sat in his royal box, and the crowd cheered. The king lowered his arm, giving the signal for the lion to be let loose. But when the lion came out into the arena, it did not attack Androclese. Instead, the lion stroked him with his paw. The lion would not hurt Androclese at all.

> The fable opens with a short description of the character, setting, and problem.

> The lion's unusual action is a hint that this might have something to do with the message or theme of the story.

This was a lion that Androclese had met and helped in the forest. All the spectators were disappointed. The king was so surprised by the behavior of the wild beast that he called to Androclese, "How did you tame this lion?" And Androclese replied, " I did not tame him, I helped him when he was in need. And now, he is showing me his gratitude."

> The theme is revealed in the dialogue between the King and Androclese.

QUESTIONS THAT HELP YOU ANALYZE THEME

1. What is the big idea or ideas?
2. What do the characters do or say about the big idea?
3. What is the writer's point or message?
4. What can the theme tell you about life?

Underline three questions you will answer about the theme. Write your answers here:

Answer ___: _____

_____

Answer ___: _____

_____

Answer ___: _____

_____

Name: _____   Date: _____

#2 Get Ready to Write: Theme

Directions

1. Think of a theme for your story. Check the theme topics in the Idea Box for help.

2. Brainstorm ideas about what your characters do or say that relates to the theme, and record them in the organizer.

IDEA BOX

childhood
courage
death
faith
family
freedom
growing up
hate
hope
patience
success
trust
truth
unhappiness
violence
war

Your ideas:

Theme Topic

What Characters Do or Say About It

| Action 1 | Action 2 | Action 3 |

Theme (What's important to learn?)

Sample Organizer

Theme Topic
Friendship/gratitude

What Characters Do or Say About It

Action 1
The lion doesn't attack Androclese— he is gentle.

Action 2
The king thinks Androclese has tamed the lion.

Action 3
Androclese explains that he didn't tame, but helped the lion when he was in need.

Theme (What's important to learn?)
Gratitude is a gift in return for a good deed.

#3 Write: Theme

Directions

1. Write a plan for your story using ideas from your organizer (page #2).
2. Use your plan to draft your story.
3. Rewrite your story using the tips below.
4. Use the checklist to make sure you've included all your ideas and polished the writing.

Plan It Out

What do you want the reader to learn from your story? _____

_____

What's the problem in your story? _____

What's the resolution to this problem? _____

What does this problem and resolution have to do with the theme? _____

_____

Write

Use the best ideas you came up with in your organizer and plan to write a first draft on lined paper.

Tip! ## Strengthening a Theme

Sample theme sentence:
But the lion did not hurt Androclese.

Sample theme sentence revised:

But when the lion came out into the arena, instead of attacking Androclese, it stroked him with his paw.

Think: How did the revised sentence add to the writing? Instead of "telling" us the lion didn't hurt Androclese, the writer revealed (or let us draw our own conclusions) the lion's unusual, caring behavior ("it stroked him with his paw").

THEME CHECKLIST

Content and Style

___ I introduce setting and characters with solid descriptions.

___ I can name the big idea or theme of my story.

___ I include actions or quotes that relate to the theme.

Mechanics

___ All of my sentences are complete.

___ I have correctly punctuated sentences and indented paragraphs.

Revise

Can you add any "show-don't-tell" details to make your theme stronger? Revise your writing on lined paper.

Short, Short Story

A short, short story is a story that embraces all of the elements of fiction—character, setting, plot, and theme—in a page or two.

Introducing the Short, Short Story

Explain to students that understanding how a short story works will help them better understand fiction writing in general. Point out that all stories have characters, a setting, a plot, and a theme, as well as three parts: a beginning, a middle, and an end. Ask students to share some favorite short stories they have read and discuss why people read short stories. Answers may include: *for enjoyment in a short period of time, to escape,* and *to connect to a character or time.*

Scaffolding Independent Writing

Post a chart in your room with questions students can use to analyze a short story.

Questions That Help Students Analyze a Short Story

- What is the setting? Does it change?
- Who is the main character? Does he or she grow or change?
- What is the problem?
- How is the problem resolved?
- What is the point the writer is making (the theme)?

Strong short, short stories can be found in teen reading magazines, such as Scholastic *Action* or *Scope* magazines. Model for students how you read and respond to a short, short story, using the questions above. Allow time for students to read a number of short, short stories and use the questions above to analyze them. You might have them use different-colored sticky notes to flag the key elements.

Tip!

Stories come together in pieces, so let students write their first drafts without self-editing. Not everything will make sense or fall into place the first time. That's okay! That is what revising is for. Peers can be very helpful in this process, letting their classmates know if the story flowed, made sense, was not too predictable, and so on.

Using the Independent Writing Activity Pages

Have students use the activity page set (pages 77–81) to practice writing their own short, short stories. Post a list of traits for a strong short story and remind students of the questions they can use to evaluate stories. Encourage them to create stories from their memories, experiences, and dreams. Young writers who follow the advice "write about what you know" usually produce their most interesting, "true," and coherent stories.

To finish up this lesson, ask students to have a classmate read their work and ask the reader: *Do you understand the story's meaning Do you follow what happened Can you describe the main character Does anything confuse you*

Name: _____   Date: _____

#1 Read and React: Short, Short Story

Directions

1. Read the model story.
2. Choose three questions about the writing to answer.

A Game to Remember

Josh had been on the bench all season. And this Friday afternoon in October was no exception. The cool wind rustled his uniform, and the air was pungent with orange slices and sports drinks. Josh loved soccer. He dreamed of playing in the World Cup one day. But his coach seemed to be happy with him just warming the bench while Alex, who was a full year older and a full head taller than Josh, played right half.

> The opening sentences set up the setting—time and place.

> This final sentence sets up the problem.

Then everything changed.

"You're in, Reynolds!" the Coach shouted at him.

"What?" Josh was in a daze, even though he had seen the whole thing. Alex ran to a ball at the sideline and collided with an opposing teammate. Blood spurted in the air as both boys fell to the ground and yellow flags flew. Broken noses.

"You are in, NOW!"

> The dialogue shows the coach's reaction to Josh.

Josh ran to the field. It was the first game he had played all season. He was shaking inside, his stomach ground his lunch like a blender. Then he ran, catching the fever. He started calling out, "free!" but the team acted as if he weren't there. No one would pass to him. Just as he was about to give up hope, a forward tripped him and he was fouled. A free kick.

> In this paragraph, the rising action brings us to the climax, or turning point.

#1 Read and React: Short, Short Story

(continued)

Josh lined up at the goal. The field was silent. All he could hear were his heavy breaths. He leaned into his cleats, mashing the earth beneath them. And then he took off, striding to the ball, lifting his leg, and kicking. The ball soared into the top corner of the net, over the goalie's head. Score!

> The climax of the story is set close to the end of the story.

It seemed like there was a brief pause before the eruption. Cheers, applause, and he was knocked to the ground by celebrating teammates. Josh had done it. He had proven himself worthy of the varsity team, and this was his moment to shine.

> The final paragraph gives the falling action, or resolution to the story.

Underline three questions you will answer about the short story. Write your answers here:

Answer ___:

_____

_____

_____

Answer ___:

_____

_____

_____

Answer ___: _____

_____

_____

> ### QUESTIONS THAT HELP YOU ANALYZE A SHORT STORY
> 1. What is the setting? Does it change?
> 2. Who is the main character? Does he or she grow or change?
> 3. What is the problem?
> 4. How is the problem resolved?
> 5. What is the point the writer is making (the theme)?

Name: _____   Date: _____

#2 Get Ready to Write: Short, Short Story

Directions

1. Think of a story idea to write about. Check the topics in the Idea Box for help.

2. Use the organizer to brainstorm details and ideas to shape a great plot.

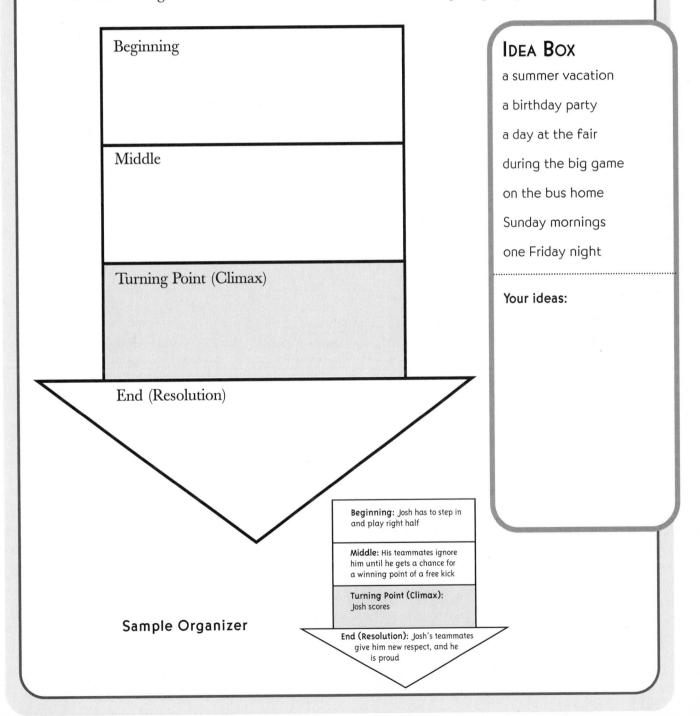

Beginning

Middle

Turning Point (Climax)

End (Resolution)

IDEA BOX

a summer vacation

a birthday party

a day at the fair

during the big game

on the bus home

Sunday mornings

one Friday night

Your ideas:

Beginning: Josh has to step in and play right half

Middle: His teammates ignore him until he gets a chance for a winning point of a free kick

Turning Point (Climax): Josh scores

End (Resolution): Josh's teammates give him new respect, and he is proud

Sample Organizer

Name: _____ Date: _____

#3 Plan: Short, Short Story

Directions

Complete the writing plan below with ideas from your organizer (page #2).

Plan It Out

Characters

Ways to describe your main character:

Physical Appearance:
- •   •
- •   •

Actions:
- •   •
- •   •

Feelings:
- •   •
- •   •

Thoughts:
- •   •
- •   •

How another character reacts to the main character:

Character 2's name: _____ reacts like this: _____

_____

Ending

Will your story's ending be a surprise? _____

Why or why not? _____

_____

Include these things in the ending that you want readers to take away:

- • _____
- • _____

Theme

Is the story's big idea or theme clear? _____

State the theme in a short sentence: _____

 Graphic Organizers and Strategy Sheets That Scaffold Writing From Paragraphs to Essays • Scholastic Teaching Resources

Name: _____   Date: _____

#4 Write: Short, Short Story

Directions

1. Use your organizer and plan (pages #2 and #3) to draft your story.

2. Rewrite your story, using the tips below.

3. Use the checklist to make sure you've included all your ideas and polished the writing.

Write a First Draft

Use the best ideas from your organizer and plan to write a first draft on lined paper.

Tip! ## Strengthening a Short, Short Story

Sample action sentence:

The coach was impatient.

Sample action sentence revised:

"You are in NOW!"

Think: How did the revised sentence add to the writing? The writer decided to use dialogue–what a character says–to reveal something (the coach's impatience) about the character.

Revise

Can you add any dialogue to make your story stronger? Revise your writing on lined paper.

SHORT, SHORT STORY CHECKLIST

Content and Style

___ I've included a beginning, a middle, and an end.

___ A clear problem is resolved.

___ The setting and characters are introduced at the beginning.

___ Several story details support my big idea.

Mechanics

___ My sentences are complete.

___ I use end marks to close each sentence.

Fable

A fable is a short, simple story that teaches a lesson. Often characters in fables are animals that talk and act like people.

Introducing the Fable

Ask students whether they've heard an adult tell a child a story that warns about something dangerous or teaches a lesson about good manners. Explain to students that this sort of moralizing story is called a fable. Emphasize that fables, like stories, have settings, characters, problems and resolutions, plots, and themes (the theme or big idea is the moral in this case). Discuss the key elements of a fable: *a simple plot, an ending with a strong moral, animal characters (personification),* and *magic numbers.*

Scaffolding Independent Writing

Post a chart in your room with questions students can use to analyze fables.

Questions That Help Students Analyze a Fable

- How is personification used?
- Who is the main character?
- What is the problem?
- How is the problem solved?
- What is the moral?

Classic Aesop fables work well because their morals are crystal clear. Model for students how you read and respond to a fable, using the questions above. Brainstorm a list of morals with students including these old standards: *slow and steady wins the race, a stitch in time saves nine,* and *do unto others as you would have done to you.* Encourage students to discuss what makes certain fables more entertaining than others. Answers may include: *funny dialogue, animals who behave like humans,* and *a surprising or satisfying ending.* Allow time for students to read a number of fables. After they have read several fables, encourage students to use the questions above to analyze them.

Using the Independent Writing Activity Pages

Have students use the activity page set (pages 83–87) to practice writing their fables. Post a list of traits for a fable, and remind students of the questions they can use to evaluate fables. Encourage students to create their stories from an important life event that has a moral they would like to share with others.

To finish up this lesson, ask students to have a classmate read their work and ask the reader: *Do you understand my story's moral Does anything confuse you*

> **Tip!**
> Before writing their fable, review the idea of personification with the class—giving human qualities to nonhuman things—for example: *the moon danced among the trees.* Encourage students to think of clichés with animals: *wise owl, lazy donkey,* and so on. Write a list on the board and then banish these overused expressions! Students should come up with personification ideas on their own.

Name: _____ Date: _____

#1 Read and React: Fable

Directions

1. Read the model fable.

2. Choose three questions to answer about the writing.

The Cat and the Mouse

Once upon a time in the small village of Eats by the blue sea, there lived a very indulgent cat, named Paddy, who loved to eat. In the morning, she followed the milkman and drank all the spilled milk; in the afternoons, she waited by the pizza shop for tossed anchovies; in the evenings she prowled family barbecues for bits of chicken or lamb. Paddy even dreamed about succulent mice and slimy fish.

> The introduction "once upon a time," signals the fable and gives us details about the setting, the main character, and her bad habit.

Then one day, on the way to the fish market, Paddy met a shimmering, golden mouse. "What a lovely mouse you are! I am going to eat you up!" Paddy licked her whiskers.

> The story introduces a magical character.

"Oh, please, do not eat me! If you do not eat me, but do as I say, you will have all the milk you need."

Paddy thought about this offer and decided it was a good one.

"Cat, you must find a mouse on the docks, carry him home, and leave him with his family."

> The task—in a set of magical threes—is presented to the cat.

"No problem," Paddy purred and headed for the docks.

On the way, her belly began to growl, and she cursed herself for making this deal. When she arrived at the docks, all the mice scattered. "Here mousies!" Paddy called. Finally she came upon a wee, baby mouse. "Oh, he looks tender!" Paddy thought. With saliva dripping from her pink mouth, Paddy pleaded, "Let me carry you home to your family, little mouse." The baby mouse looked up innocently, smiled, and shook his head: *yes.*

> The action moves along, showing how the cat completes the task.

Name: _____   Date: _____

#1 Read and React: Fable

(continued)

Paddy bent down and carried the mouse by the neck, as if it were a kitten. She could taste how yummy it would be, but she resisted the little snack for the promised milk. Once at the mouse's hole, she left the baby at the door. The mouse's family stared through their window in disbelief as Paddy walked away.

"Okay, golden mouse!" Paddy mewed. "I did it!"

"Well done!" cried the mouse, appearing from the darkness. And here is your milk. A single small bowl of milk appeared at Paddy's feet.

> Here comes the climax, the turning point of the fable.

"What is this?" she cried. "Where is all the milk I could want?"

"Oh, no, Ms. Cat. I said all the milk a cat would need." And with that, he disappeared.

> The moral: We should be content with only what we need.

Just as Paddy was getting mad, the tiny mouse appeared, bringing her a crumble of cheese. Paddy licked it up, smiled at the mouse, and knew she had made the right decision.

> Both the mouse and the cat are satisfied—a better ending.

Underline three questions you will answer about the fable. Write your answers here:

Answer ___: _____

_____

Answer ___: _____

_____

_____

Answer ___: _____

_____

_____

> ## QUESTIONS THAT HELP YOU ANALYZE A FABLE
> 1. How is personification used?
> 2. Who is the main character?
> 3. What is the problem?
> 4. How is the problem solved?
> 5. What is the moral?

#2 Get Ready to Write: Fable

Directions

1. Choose a moral for a story that interests you. Check the Idea Box for help.

2. Fill in the organizer with your ideas.

Character (Hero or Heroine)		
Tasks the Character Must Complete		
1	2	3

Problem

What the Character Learns (Moral)

How the Character Changes

Sample Organizer

IDEA BOX

might doesn't always make right

slow and steady wins the race

friendship is precious

don't trust strangers

do unto others as you would have done to you

it's better to give than to receive

- - - - - - - - - - - - - -

Your ideas:

Character (Hero or Heroine) a cat, Paddy		
Tasks the Character Must Complete		
1. cat must find a mouse	2. carry it home	3. walk away

Problem Must make the mouse believe she will not hurt it; must not eat the mouse!

What the Character Learns (Moral)
self-control is one key to success

How the Character Changes
learns that waiting is a virtue

Name: _____   Date: _____

#3 Plan: Fable

Directions

Complete the writing plan using the tips below and the ideas from your organizer (page #2).

(Tip!) **Three Characteristics of Fables to Try Out**

1. **Personify:** Give human qualities (like speech and feeling) to things that are not human.

   Example: *A greedy cat and a golden mouse both speak and experience feelings in the same way humans do.*

2. **Add elements of magic, including fantastical creatures:** A magical or evil force may work against the hero or heroine, forcing him or her to rise to a challenge. Unusual creatures may appear, such as fairies or elves, that may come to the aid of the hero or heroine.

   Examples: *The cat must resist all temptation to eat the golden mouse and the baby mouse and instead bring the baby mouse home. The golden, shimmering mouse is an unusual creature.*

3. **Use magic numbers:** Things occur in threes, sevens, or elevens.

   Example: *The cat must perform three tasks to earn her milk.*

Plan It Out

Personification

Will you use animal characters? _____ If so, which human qualities will you give them?

Character 1 _____ Human qualities: _____

Character 2 _____ Human qualities: _____

Character 3 _____ Human qualities: _____

Magical Numbers

What numbers are important in your fable? _____ Why? _____

_____

Elements of Magic and Fantastical Characters

Ideas for including surprising elements in your fable: _____

_____

Name: _____   Date: _____

#4 Write: Fable

Directions

1. Write a draft of your fable using your organizer and plan (pages #2 and #3).

2. Use the tips below to improve and rewrite your fable.

3. Use the checklist to make sure you've included all your ideas and polished the writing.

Write a First Draft

Use the best ideas from your organizer and plan to write a first draft on lined paper.

(Tip!) Strengthening a Fable

Sample sentence:

The magic mouse begged the cat for mercy.

Sample sentence revised:

"Oh please, lovely cat, do not eat me! If you do not eat me, but do as I say, you will have all the milk a kitty could need."

Think: How did the revised sentence add to the writing? The writer decided to use dialogue—what a mouse says to the cat—to reveal two things:

- flattery helps the mouse appeal to the cat (he calls the cat "lovely") and

- the mouse's promise of a reward ("all the milk a kitty could need") sets a great challenge for the cat.

Revise

Can you add any dialogue to make your story stronger? Revise your writing on lined paper.

FABLE CHECKLIST

Content and Style

___ My fable has a beginning, middle, and end.

___ A mean-spirited or evil force is present.

___ I've introduced and described the setting and a hero (main character).

___ I've included important numbers, such as a set of three things.

___ Some events are solved by magic.

___ I've stated a clear moral of the story at the end.

___ I used personification effectively.

Mechanics

___ I have complete sentences.

CHAPTER 4

Revising and Editing

"It's fine the way it is!" "I like the way it sounds." Have you heard those comments before? Revising and editing are probably the most difficult steps for young writers. Rethinking and restructuring a piece of writing to make it better is a hard concept for students who have spent time on a draft. Teaching students strategies to revisit their work—and giving them time to do so—is key to making revision and editing a comfortable part of the writing process for students. The organizers in this section help students focus on several different aspects of revision—so they can become critical readers of their own writing.

To help students, create a poster with these tips to hang in your room:

Revising and Editing Tips

- Review your draft—star the parts that work and check the parts that need to be changed.
- Ask questions about parts to generate more details.
- Add, cut, rearrange, and reword. Be specific and clear so you don't leave your reader with any confusion.
- Go back and pay special attention to the opening and closing. Are they strong enough?
- Shape up your style. Does the writing sound interesting and natural? Do you use colorful, sensory words?
- Get an opinion from a peer.

Lessons in This Section

- Revision
- Editing
- Spotting an Error
- Using Editor's Symbols
- Language and Style
- Creating a Rubric

Revision

Revision is reworking writing until all the parts work equally well. Make sure to emphasize to students that revision is not punishment; it's all about improving writing. Revision, like writing, is an ongoing process that takes time.

Introducing Revision

Introduce students to the concept of revision by asking them what would happen if a writer never reread his or her own writing? Their answers might include: *the writing would have a lot of mistakes and things would not make sense.* Explain that writing is not a one-time act and that rewriting allows writers to improve their work. You might compare rewriting to the tablespoon of baking powder you add to a cake's batter. It looks like a small amount, but without it the cake—or writing—would be flat.

Scaffolding Independent Writing

Post a chart in your room with questions students can use to aid in the revision process.

Questions That Help Students Revise

- Have I answered the questions asked?
- Do I back up each point with an example?
- Have I been specific?
- Does the writing sound like me? Is it personal or too businesslike?
- What makes my writing memorable?

Before students revise on their own, model how you read and revise a piece of writing using the questions above. Think aloud about what needs to be changed.

Using the Independent Writing Activity Pages

Have the students use the activity page set (pages 90–92) to practice revising on their own.

- **Before revision:** Before students jump into revising a piece, tell them to put the writing they plan to rework in their folders and let it sit for a few days. That way, they can get some distance from it—and return to it with fresh eyes. In the meantime, students can go back to other writing pieces or begin a new project.

- **During revision:** Providing feedback to a writer is critical to helping him or her improve the work. Have students read their piece aloud to you or to a peer group. After reading, confer (or have peer-groups confer) with each student about what worked and what changes might help the piece. Encourage students to use the questions that you or their peers have asked when making their revisions. Then, have them rewrite parts, seek more feedback, and apply those ideas to their writing.

- **After revision:** When students feel that they have finished revising a piece, confer with them again. Some students will need more guidance than others. Let students hear your thinking process for how you might go about rewriting a lead or improving details.

To finish up the lesson, ask students to discuss (in pairs, as a whole class, or in a one-on-one conference): *Why is revision important to my writing?*

Name: _____ Date: _____

#1 Read and React: Revision

Directions

1. Read the before-and-after models.

2. Choose two questions to answer about the writing.

Model

Before: I put the grill away. I grill corn and chicken. I get the grill out. I am careful when I clean it and turn it on. I place the food on the grill in horizontal lines. I scrape off anything that has burned.

After: When it is time to make dinner on summer evenings, I carefully roll out the gas grill from the backyard shed. I first clean it by scraping off any burned food that may have been left on from the last time I grilled. Then, very gingerly, I light the grill. Mom has prepared chicken and corn, which I place on the grill in horizontal lines. I have to be very watchful the whole time I am grilling so that I do not burn myself or the food. I place the food on the platter, turn off the grill, clean it, and roll it away. After all, as my father always says, "no job is done until the cleanup is finished." Finally, we all enjoy a savory supper.

> This sentence gives us a time and a place.

> The author shows order using time-order words.

> Specific nouns—*corn* instead of *food*—add interest.

> A quote helps describe an attitude about cleaning up instead of just telling about it.

QUESTIONS THAT HELP YOU REVISE

1. Has the writer backed up each point with an example?

2. Has he or she been specific?

3. Does the writing sound "real"? Is it personal or too businesslike?

4. What makes the writing memorable?

Underline two questions that you will answer about the model revision. Write your answers here:

Answer ___: _____

_____

_____

Answer ___: _____

_____

_____

#2 Get Ready to Revise

Directions

1. Read the revision tips below.

2. Practice your revision skills with the before-and-after examples.

Tips! ## Revision

Let your writing sit: With a little distance from your writing, you will spot clunky sentences more quickly.

Get an attention-grabbing topic: Is the content worth sharing? Make sure the content is interesting and the style is natural, so your real message will be clear.

Rewrite parts: Don't jump into the whole piece headfirst; it may be too much. Select a sentence or two and start there.

Ask questions: Ask about an idea, a word, or a sentence. Make sure you can prove that it is worth keeping in your writing. What questions did the revised writing answer about the first draft? What details make the writing crystal clear? What words or phrases showed you specific actions or things in the writing?

Practice

Use the revision tips to revise a title, lead, and description:

Draft title: *My Summer Swimming*
Revised title: *A July Splashing Up Fun*

Your turn: _____

Draft lead: *I never went in the water much before this summer but I liked it.*
Revised lead: *I swam so much this summer at Lake Jade, I think I grew fins.*

Your turn: _____

_____

Draft description: *The water is okay.*
Revised description: *Lake water is green, dense, cool, and smells fresh—perfect for playing get-away from my cousins.*

Your turn: _____

_____

Name: _____   Date: _____

#3 Perform: Revision

Directions

1. Select a piece of your writing to revise.

2. Then, make a revision plan for your writing. Use the Revision Tips (page #2), as well.

3. Use the checklist to make sure you have thoroughly revised your piece.

Plan It Out

Title of the piece you want to revise: _____

Does your title grab the reader's attention? _____

Revision ideas for the title: _____

_____

Here are two sentences that need more details or leave readers with unanswered questions:

● _____

● _____

Rewrite these sentences, adding or cutting information to make them clearer:

● _____

_____

● _____

_____

What thoughts did you leave readers with?

_____

_____

What more can you add or cut? _____

_____

_____

> ### REVISION CHECKLIST
>
> ___ I've added descriptive details to create a clearer picture for the reader.
>
> ___ I've answered questions the reader might bring up.
>
> ___ I have a snappy title.
>
> ___ I've cut any unnecessary information that did not support the topic.

Editing

While revision has to do with content, editing has to do with style, organization, and conventions. One thing that has helped me when I conduct writing workshop is to make revising and editing two distinct stages. When students are asked to do everything at once, they become overwhelmed.

Introducing Editing

Explain that all writers need guidelines before they begin to write. Ask students to help you come up with a rubric or criteria list for what must be included in their writing. Establishing criteria in this way not only gives students a map and a destination for their writing, it also give them ownership of the process. You may have to help students adapt their criteria for different genres.

Scaffolding Editing

Post a chart in your room with questions students can use to edit.

Questions That Help Students Edit

- Does the organization make sense?
- Are my sentences complete?
- Have I slashed, squeezed, and straightened my sentences?
- Are words capitalized and spelled correctly?
- Have I used punctuation marks correctly and effectively?
- (You may want to add specific criteria for the type of piece students are editing.)

Before students begin to edit, model for them how you edit a piece of writing, using the questions above. Think aloud about how you catch mistakes. Encourage students to edit for one criterion at a time. Feedback will be crucial for your students' success. You can arm them with suggestions for improving their writing.

Using the Independent Writing Activity Pages

Have the students use the activity page set (pages 94–96) to practice editing on their own. Keep the criteria list posted and remind students to refer to the questions they worked with to practice editing. If you notice that certain students are having trouble mastering a specific criterion–run-on sentences, for example–you can present a mini-lesson to them to reinforce the skill. Encourage students to allow a peer to read their piece or to reread their writing aloud in order to catch anything that may have slipped by.

To finish up the lesson, ask students to take some time to reflect on what they've learned about editing. Discuss (in pairs, as a whole class, or in a one-on-one conference): *How do revision and editing differ*

Name: _____ Date: _____

#1 Read and React: Editing

Directions

1. Study the three S's: Slash, Straighten, and Squeeze.

2. Read the before-and-after models and notice which S's the editor used.

 Tip! Editing

Use three S's when you edit:

- **Slash:** If a section of writing seems like it is not necessary or is too wordy, take it out.
- **Straighten:** If something is unclear or confusing to you or your reader, find the problem phrase and reorganize it.
- **Squeeze:** If some writing is too long and repetitive, rewrite it so it is simple and clear.

Models

Before: I live in Springfield Ohio, since I was fourteen on September 14 1994.

After: I have lived in Springfield, Ohio, since my fourteenth birthday on September 14, 1994.

> STRAIGHTEN! Notice how the writer adds commas and fixes the verb tense.

Before: I think windy days like last Friday or remember last Saturday are the best. At four, when it is windy in the afternoon I liked to go out and fly my kite. I throw paper airplanes in the backyard and chase swirling leaves.

After: I think windy days like last Friday are the best. In the afternoon, when it is windy, I like to go out and fly my kite. Other things I like to do in the backyard when it is windy are throwing paper airplanes and chasing swirling leaves.

> SLASH! No need to mention all of your thoughts.

> SQUEEZE! No need to repeat the times "at four" and "in the afternoon."

> STRAIGHTEN! Show that these are other things you do when it's windy.

Name: _____   Date: _____

#2 Get Ready to Edit

Directions

1. Review the models on page #1.

2. Choose a piece of your writing and follow the directions for editing it.

3. Choose two questions about your writing to answer.

Title of the piece to edit: _____

Choose two of your sentences to slash, straighten, or squeeze.

Before: _____

_____

_____

After: _____

_____

_____

Before: _____

_____

_____

After: _____

_____

_____

Underline two questions you will answer about your writing. Write your answers here:

Answer ___: _____

_____

_____

Answer ___: _____

_____

_____

QUESTIONS THAT HELP YOU EDIT

1. Does the organization make sense?

2. Are my sentences complete? Punctuated correctly?

3. Are words capitalized? Spelled correctly?

4. Do I have a lead and a conclusion?

5. Other criteria: _____

_____

Name: _____ Date: _____

#3 Edit

Directions

1. Using the piece you have selected, answer the questions below about your writing.

2. Use the checklist to make sure you have thoroughly edited your piece.

Editing Plan

Use this list as a guide when you edit your writing. You can add other criteria that you are working on for a specific piece of writing:

Sentence Structure

My sentences are clear and complete.   Yes   No   Notes:

Punctuation, Capitalization, Spelling

Each sentence ends with a punctuation mark.   Yes   No   Notes:

All my sentences start with a capital letter.   Yes   No   Notes:

I've checked words I was unsure how to spell.   Yes   No   Notes:

Slash, Straighten, Squeeze

I've removed unnecessary details or phrases.   Yes   No   Notes:

I've reorganized my writing to make it clear.

Yes   No   Notes:

I've replaced wordy sections with simple, clear writing.

Yes   No   Notes:

EDITING CHECKLIST

____ I've read my final draft aloud.
____ Each sentence is clearly written.
____ The writing is clear, not too wordy.
____ I've replaced awkward or confusing words or phrases.
____ I've checked spelling, commas, and end punctuation.

Spotting an Error

Students find it difficult and often overwhelming to edit a piece for more than one convention at a time. This lesson offers suggestions for helping students break down the process into manageable parts.

Introducing Error Spotting

Use the criteria list students helped develop in the editing lesson (see page 93) or have them come up with a specific rubric or criteria list for editing new pieces of writing. Tell them that editors often check a piece for one or two types of errors at a time. If they search for too many things at once, they can miss important problems that need to be fixed.

Scaffolding Error Spotting

Post a chart in your room with questions students can use to spot errors.

Questions That Help Students Spot an Error:

- Are all sentences complete?
- Is the punctuation correct?
- Are words capitalized?
- Have I checked the spelling of difficult words?
- Do the sentences flow?

Before students spot specific errors, model for them how you use this editing strategy with a piece of writing, using the questions above. Show them how to catch mistakes by reading the piece backward (this helps them slow down and focus on each sentence). Model how you edit for one element at a time—you can use different-colored pens to mark different elements. Then, have students work with your assistance on another one of their pieces. (Always do editing in class so that you can be there to support their work.)

After one round of editing, offer feedback. When students become successful at spotting errors, they get excited. And the more errors that students can spot and correct, the more they learn about editing. Have students edit for only those criteria that you set and search for one element at a time (for example, if you set three criteria, students should read through their writing three times).

Using the Independent Writing Activity Pages

Have students use the activity page set (pages 98–100) to practice spotting errors on their own. Keep the criteria list posted and remind students to refer to the questions they worked with to practice editing. Encourage students to allow a peer to read their piece or to reread their writing aloud in order to catch anything that may have slipped by.

To finish up the lesson, ask students to discuss (in pairs, as a whole class, or in a one-on-one conference): *What are my best strategies for spotting errors in my own writing*

> **Tip!**
> Students may not "get" the editing process immediately. It takes repeated practice. Make it a part of the writing process—and not a hurried afterthought—and your students will approach revision with gusto.

#1 Read and React: Spotting an Error

Directions

1. Read aloud (but to yourself) the before-and-after model, marking errors that you find.
2. Choose two questions to answer about the writing.

Model

Before

About three years ago a new gym was built in neighborhood. Its not in walking distance of my house which is not good. The problem is all the effort of getting a ride. My parents are busy. "joe, my father said to me yesterday, " you've got to understand that both your mother and me work."

After

About three years ago a new gym was built in my neighborhood. It's not in walking distance of my house, which is not good. The problem is it takes a lot of effort to get a ride. My parents are busy. "Joe," my father said to me yesterday, "you've got to understand that both your mother and I work."

Add missing pronouns.

Use a comma to set off this clause.

Use correct capitalization and punctuation of a direct quote.

Insert an apostrophe

Make the sentence complete.

Use the correct pronoun reference.

QUESTIONS THAT HELP YOU SPOT AN ERROR

1. Which sentence was incomplete in the first draft?
2. What punctuation did I have to correct?
3. Which words needed to be capitalized?
4. Which words have I checked for spelling errors?
5. How can I make the sentences flow?

Underline two questions you will answer about your editing work. Write your answers here:

Answer ___: _____

_____

_____

Answer ___: _____

_____

_____

Name: _____   Date: _____

#2 Get Ready to Spot an Error

Directions

1. Read the tips for spotting errors in your writing.

2. Try your hand at editing the piece of writing below.

(Tips!) Easily Spot Errors

Read your piece aloud: You will catch small mistakes and hear whether the content holds together and makes sense.

Ask questions: Ask whether everything is clear. Ask about paragraphs, complete sentences, punctuation, and spelling.

Rework the writing: Make changes until it works the way you want it to.

Get an editing partner: Find a classmate to proofread your piece (make a final check for mistakes) while you proofread his or her piece.

Model

Vacation is always an adventure. Last summer I went to Ocean city Maryland with my family. We stayed at a nice Hotel for ten days. On the fifth day my brother and I found a turtle and we brought it back to our hotel room. My mother was not plesed. My father said we could keep him. I named him sandy in honor of our trip

Your edited version:

_____

_____

_____

_____

_____

_____

_____

_____

Use this checklist to make sure you found all of the errors in the model.

____ I found three capitalization mistakes.

____ I found one missing end mark.

____ I inserted three commas.

____ I corrected one misspelled word.

____ I gave the piece a title.

Name: _____ Date: _____

#3 Perform: Spot an Error

Directions

1. Using a piece of writing you have selected, answer the questions below.
2. Use the checklist to make sure you have thoroughly edited your piece.

Questions to Ask Yourself About Your Writing

What punctuation, capitalization, spelling, or usage mistakes do I most often make?

Punctuation

- _____
- _____
- _____
- _____

Capitalization

- _____
- _____
- _____
- _____

Spelling

- _____
- _____
- _____
- _____

Usage

- _____
- _____
- _____
- _____

SPOTTING AN ERROR CHECKLIST

___ I have headed my page and given the piece a title.

___ All sentences are complete and have end punctuation.

___ I have used commas correctly.

___ I have punctuated quotations properly.

___ I have checked the spelling of words I am unsure of.

___ All sentences and proper nouns begin with a capital letter.

Editing Symbols

Professional editors use specific symbols to mark up texts for revision and editing. Though your red pen may be itching to edit student papers, putting the cap back on and teaching students to recognize and fix errors in basic conventions can save time.

Introducing Editing Symbols

Explain to students that the final stage of editing is proofreading, or reviewing your edited piece to check for any mistakes that might make your writing hard to read. Introduce students to proofreading with editing symbols by asking, *When you proofread what do you look for* Their answers may include: *capitalization, punctuation,* and *spelling.* Discuss the importance of proofreading to fix errors and create an error-free final draft. Next, show an overhead transparency of page 102 (basic editing symbols) and discuss their meanings with students: *indents, add punctuation, add a word, fix spelling, add a capital letter, add a lowercase letter, move,* and *take out.*

Have students follow along as you correct the sample paragraph at the bottom of the page together. As students volunteer corrections, mark the symbols and corrections on the transparency. The edited copy should look like this:

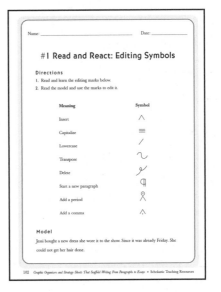

Jessi bought a new dress she wore it to the show. Since it was already Friday, She could not get her hair done.

Model the procedure with additional sample paragraphs until students are comfortable with recognizing errors and making corrections.

Using the Independent Writing Activity Pages

Have students use the activity page set (pages 102–103) to practice marking the symbols on their own. The corrected sentences should look like this:

1. After a long time, I heard her heavy footsteps echoing in the halls of castle bundalee.

2. after all this time, I cant believe I still remember the story like it was yesterday?

3. jack went home, he was still late for his Basketball practice.

4. Near the stream in the Woods is a vine, That you can swing on.

At the end of the activity (bottom of page 103), students will need to select a piece of their own to proofread. They can use red pens and their editing symbols sheet to go through the writing sample, making corrections where necessary. Encourage students to reread their writing aloud or allow a peer to read their piece in order to catch anything that may have slipped by.

To finish up the lesson, ask students to discuss (in pairs, as a whole class, or in a one-on-one conference): *Which symbols do I usually use to edit my writing   Which do I need to learn*

#1 Read and React: Editing Symbols

Directions

1. Read and learn the editing marks below.
2. Read the model and use the marks to edit it.

Meaning	Symbol
Insert	$\wedge$
Capitalize	$\equiv$
Lowercase	/
Transpose	$\sim$
Delete	
Start a new paragraph	¶
Add a period	$\odot$
Add a comma	$\wedge$

Model

Jessi bought a new dress she wore it to the show. Since it was already Friday. She could not get her hair done.

#2 Practice: Editing Symbols

Directions

1. Use the editing symbols to mark errors in the sentences below. Write the corrected sentences on the lines provided.

2. Select a paragraph of your own writing and proofread it using the editing marks (page #1).

Edit

Practice marking the editing symbols on these sentences.

1. After a long time I heard her hevy footsteps echoing in the halls of castle bundalee

   _____

   _____

2. after all this time I cant believe I still rememberer the story like it was yesterday?

   _____

   _____

3. jack went home he was still late for his Basketball practice.

   _____

   _____

4. Near the stream in the Woods is a vine. That you can swing on.

   _____

   _____

After you've proofread your own piece, recopy the polished version here:

_____

_____

_____

_____

_____

_____

Language and Style

Style is the way in which the writer uses words, phrases, or sentences to form ideas. Style can also be the qualities—or language—that one writer uses to distinguish his or her writing from another's. For example, students will recognize that R.L. Stine writes in a completely different style than Gary Paulsen does.

Introducing Language and Style

Discuss with students what style means. Some people wear their hair short, others long. Some people like to tuck in their shirts, while others leave them out. Your style depends on your tastes. The same goes for writing. Explain to students that the more you write, the more you develop a personal style.

Scaffolding Independent Writing

Before diving into a lesson on writing style, guide students to notice the ways in which different published authors write. The best way to learn about different styles is to have students model their writing after someone else's. This is not plagiarism—students are not copying a writer's ideas or words, but the flow, sound, and pattern of the sentences. Evaluate with students how professional writers use the following stylistic elements:

- Formal versus informal language—the language can be distant and sound free of personal bias, or it can sound like a conversation with a friend.

- Point of view—some writers use the first-person voice ("I"), while others use third-person voice ("he/she"). Sometimes the first-person voice makes readers more comfortable because the writer speaks directly to them.

- Word choice—selecting just the right words helps authors describe precisely and can give the piece rhythm and flow.

- Literary elements—techniques such as metaphors and similes, foreshadowing, and alliteration make key ideas memorable.

Model for students how you might use the style of a famous line of poetry to begin your own poem. Encourage students to sample many different writers' styles before deciding on their own.

Using the Independent Writing Activity Pages

Have students use the activity page set (pages 105–107) to practice crafting their language and style on their own. Post the examples and remind students to refer to them as they try out different styles. Encourage students to read their writing aloud in order to catch any lapses in style.

To finish up the lesson, ask students to discuss (in pairs, as a whole class, or in a one-on-one conference): *How does my writing show my personal style*

Getting at Writing Style

- Discuss with students the following terms: *point of view, diction, slang, informal writing,* and *semiformal writing.*

- Brainstorm with students different kinds of writing (an e-mail from a friend, a news or magazine article, a book of jokes, a speech written 100 years ago, and so forth) that may use these elements of style in different ways.

- Start a chart in your classroom and allow students to add to the chart as they come up with different kinds of writing.

- Copy a few different short pieces from magazines—editorials, letters, articles, sidebars—and distribute them to groups. Have the groups read the pieces and identify the style elements that the writer used.

Name: _____ Date: _____

#1 Read and React: Language and Style

Directions

1. Read the before-and-after model.
2. Choose two questions about the writing to answer.

Model

Before: It was a pretty day as I walked along the skyline drive. It was a good name for a park because on top of the mountains I felt like I could touch the sky. I wanted to be alone to think about things. I walked along a path to a brook. I sat down and almost dozed off listening to interesting sounds.

After: The sun shone, sparkling on the maple trees. Sweat glistened on my neck as I hiked up the skyline drive. The trails edge the top of the Blue Ridge Mountains, giving the park its unusual name. Times that I need to think about big decisions like what to do this summer, I come up to these trails to be alone with my thoughts. Today, I walked along the path to Solomon's Brook, eyeing all of the wildflowers and blue beetles. After my trek, I sat on a cool rock and dangled my feet in the water. All around me bees hummed, birds twitted, and the wind rushed through branches. It was a natural lullaby.

Underline two questions you will answer about your style work. Write your answers here:

Answer ___: _____

_____

_____

Answer ___: _____

_____

_____

QUESTIONS THAT HELP YOU THINK ABOUT STYLE

1. Which language is formal? Which is informal?
2. What point of view does the writer use?
3. Does the point of view make the writing sound familiar or reporter-like?
4. What words seem carefully chosen?
5. Can you spot a metaphor? How does it make this piece stronger?

#2 Understand Language and Style

Directions

1. Read the notes about word choice and style in the box.

2. Practice revising for language and style on the sentences below.

3. Select a piece of your own writing to revise for language and style.

Diction in writing refers to the language or word choice that you use. Your words should match your purpose:

- A story set in a specific place might call for *slang* or *dialect*.

- A character sketch might call for *informal English*—and contain contractions and popular expressions (*you know, forget it, no way*).

- Most essays use *semiformal English* writing that contains more carefully chosen words.

Tell what kind of diction the writer is using and circle the evidence in the sentence.

Most students will enjoy this experiment. _____

I heard something that got my attention._____

"Y'all come back now, you hear!" _____

Style is the way you use words, phrases, and sentences in your own special way to express your ideas. But to make your style enjoyable for your reader, make sure your writing is

- **Focused:** The writing shows purpose. It uses one word when one word will do.

- **Solid as stone:** The writing shows precision and color. It lets the reader see, hear, and feel.

- **Active:** The writing shows life and energy.

- **One of a kind:** The writing is original.

Choose a piece of your own writing to edit for language and style.

Title of your piece:_____. What elements of style will you add or improve?: _____

_____

Name: _____ Date: _____

#3 Revise: Language and Style

Directions

1. Now you are ready to revise your own writing for diction and style. Choose three sentences from your writing to revise below.

2. Use the checklist to guide your full revision.

A) My sentence before: _____

_____

Hint: Read the sentence aloud. Is it focused? Rewrite the sentence making sure to use only one word when one word will do.

After: _____

_____

_____

B) My sentence before: _____

_____

Hint: Read the sentence aloud. Is it solid? Rewrite the sentence, making sure to use language with precision and color. Let the reader see, hear, and feel what you're writing about.

After: _____

_____

_____

C) My sentence before: _____

_____

Hint: Read the sentence aloud. Is it active? Rewrite the sentence making sure to write with life and energy.

After:_____

_____

_____

CHECKLIST FOR STYLE

___ I've combined many short sentences into smoother reading sentences.

___ All my sentences are active! I've changed all passive verbs to active ones.

___ I've used the right diction for formal or informal language.

___ I've used repetition appropriately: for rhythm, balance, effect, and unity.

Creating a Rubric

A rubric is a scoring guide used in qualitative assessments (writing). A rubric outlines the criteria for a piece of writing and presents a corresponding rating scale. A scoring rubric makes clear the expected qualities of performance on a rating scale.

Introducing Rubrics

Ask students what they know about rubrics and how they are helpful. Their answers may include: *they are charts with numbers to show how well you do your work* and *they let me know what to check for.*

Scaffolding Independent Writing

Model for students how you would use a rubric in revising or editing a piece of writing. Teachers and students can establish expectations for their work and then use the rubric to evaluate the final draft. Give students a chance to practice using a rubric on other students' writing (make sure to ask for the writers' permission and cover their names when you present the writing). Once students are comfortable with using the rubrics, they can use them to evaluate their own writing. Encourage students to be a part of the process of making criteria for each graded writing piece. Print up the criteria on a chart in the room so that students can have it as another reference.

> **Tip!**
> The rubric on page 109 can be used to evaluate many papers throughout the year. Just adapt the criteria with your students so that the rubric applies to the genre you've assigned. Working through the criteria with students will help them learn the elements of writing that are common to good writing in any genre, as well as those elements that are specific to particular genres.

Using the Independent Writing Activity Pages

Have students use activity page 109 to practice using rubrics on their own. Copy the rubric page and hand it out to students before they revise their writing. The criteria you will use to grade their writing should not be a mystery to them. Knowing the criteria will help students write and revise. Keep the criteria posted and remind students to refer to them as they edit. Encourage students to read their writing aloud in order to catch any problems. At the end, students should have a clear, fluid piece.

To finish up the lesson, ask students to discuss (in pairs, as a whole class, or in a one-on-one conference): *How is using a rubric helpful when I revise*

Name: _____ Date: _____

#1 Create a Rubric

Directions

1. Now you are ready to create your own grading guidelines for a piece of writing.

2. At the end of each section, add one or two additional traits you think your piece of writing should contain.

3. After writing, go back and check against your rubric to make sure you have met your goals.

	Off-Track	Right-On	Outstanding
Style & Organization Sentences are varied. Verbs are strong. Language suits purpose/genre.			
Slash/Straighten/Squeeze The writing is not too wordy. No unnecessary information remains. The organization makes sense.			
Content The topic is not stale. The purpose is clear. The title is short and snappy.			
Mechanics: Punctuation, Capitalization, Spelling All sentences have end punctuation. All sentences begin with capital letters. All words are spelled correctly. Paragraphs are indented.			
Other Traits			

Resources

Action magazine (Scholastic, monthly issues).

Canfield, J. et al. (2000). *Chicken soup for the preteen soul: 101 stories of change, choices, and growing up for kids ages 9–12.* Deerfield Beach, FL: Health Communications, Inc.

Munsch, R. N. (2002, reprint). *The paper bag princess.* Toronto: Annick Press.

Scope magazine (Scholastic, 16 issues yearly).

Sizoo, B. (2001). *Teaching powerful writing.* New York: Scholastic.

Taylor, T. (1969). *The cay.* New York: Dell Yearling Books.

Weatherford, C. B. (2005). *Freedom on the menu: The Greensboro sit-ins.* New York: Dial Books for Young Readers.

Index

Index